# THE CHANCE
# TO SURVIVE

## LAWRENCE ALDERSON

PILKINGTON PRESS

DEDICATION

*To Rebecca and Daniel*

*custodians of our heritage in the next generation*

PUBLISHED BY:
PILKINGTON PRESS LTD
YELVERTOFT MANOR
YELVERTOFT
NORTHAMPTONSHIRE NN6 7LF

© LAWRENCE ALDERSON 1978, 1989, 1994

FIRST PUBLISHED 1978 CAMERON & TAYLEUR
FIRST REVISED EDITION 1989 A.H. JOLLY (EDITORIAL) LTD
SECOND REVISED EDITION 1994 PILKINGTON PRESS LTD

ISBN 1 899044 06 X Paper bound edition
ISBN 1 899044 07 8 Case bound edition

PRODUCED, DESIGNED AND TYPESET BY:
A.H. JOLLY (EDITORIAL) LTD
YELVERTOFT MANOR
NORTHAMPTONSHIRE NN6 7LF

PRINTED BY:
SNOECK DUCAJU & ZOON. BELGIUM

COVER ILLUSTRATION: WILD CATTLE OF CHILLINGHAM
BY PERMISSION OF LAING ART GALLERY,
NEWCASTLE UPON TYNE (TYNE AND WEAR MUSEUMS)

# CONTENTS

# LIST OF ILLUSTRATIONS
## and Photographic Acknowledgements

# INTRODUCTION

The basic principles and policies of genetic conservation of domestic livestock, that were established in the 1970s and detailed in the first edition of this book, still hold good today. On the other hand, the programmes and procedures required to implement those policies are changing at an ever increasing rate and new concepts are emerging continually. Thus, although this edition still rests on the firm bedrock of a tried and tested philosophy, it had become necessary to record the wide variety of significant changes and developments which have taken place in the last five years.

Changes in the Priority Lists of the Rare Breeds Survival Trust are a good indicator of the general situation, and they provide evidence of a dynamic situation. Even in the interval between the completion of the revision of the text and the publication of this book, another breed, the Balwen from Wales, had been added to the Lists, closely following its compatriot breed the Hill Radnor. Looking ahead only a little way, it is possible that the Lists may be augmented even further by breeds such as Llanwenog, Kerry Hill, South Wales Mountain, Devon and Cornwall Longwool, Whitefaced Dartmoor and Dorset Down sheep, Devon and Lincoln Red cattle and others. All these breeds are in a vulnerable state and continue to decline as other breeds, including many imported breeds, increasingly dominate the livestock industry.

On the other hand, we can point with undisguised pride and pleasure to the improved status of all breeds on the Lists, and to breeds such as Jacob, Black Welsh Mountain and Lleyn sheep, which not only have graduated from the Priority Lists but also have now left even the Minority List and become fully fledged mainstream members of the sheep industry. We trust that others will follow. Already breeds such as Oxford Down sheep, Dexter cattle and Shire horses have reached the Minority List, and others such as Hebridean sheep and British White cattle show every indication of doing so in the near future. In this see-saw of fluctuating fortunes, the underlying satisfaction, but not complacency, is that no more breeds are being lost. We hope that extinction has become a redundant word among British rare breeds.

The programme of conservation is expanding continually and accelerating in pace. The succeeding revisions of this book have illustrated how the infectious activity has spread to all parts of the world since the late 1970s, and yet Britain remains a vital and potent source of development and change. After a brief period of 'containment' in the late 1980s, a wider vision and growth philosophy has been restored and has seen, for example, the inclusion of poultry in the programmes of the Rare Breeds Survival Trust and a more vigorous proactive attitude. A reactive, reflex response to problems is regrettably of little value in the face of a *fait accompli*.

This growth has been reflected on a wider front. Many countries have now established national conservation programmes and have joined the 'rare breeds' movement; indeed, this book has played its part in the growth of international interest. The first edition provided the stimulus for the formation of organisations in several countries, including Spain and Switzerland, which themselves are now becoming leading players on the world stage. The international status of the movement was confirmed by the creation in 1991 of a global co-ordinating organisation, Rare Breeds International, of which I have the privilege to be the Founder Chairman. This provides a platform to influence policy at a higher level, and I have also had the opportunity to make further direct contributions to the support of conservation programmes through EC-sponsored studies of endangered breeds of livestock in Europe and as a member of the Working Party of the Animal Genetic Data Bank in Hannover. This is some indication of the tempo of change and growth in the last few years.

Other less welcome factors also have served to remind us that we are all part of one global family. The recent economic recession has not been inhibited by national boundaries, while the ever increasing and voluminous EC legislation arouses passion of varying allegiance in all parts of Europe. 'Political' negotiations and manoeuvres may be resented as diversions from the real task of genetic conservation, but they are inevitable and increasingly essential. A powerful lobbying facility can have valuable and important effects, and several EC Directives have reflected the influence of our conservation lobby. It is hoped that Rare Breeds International will widen this impact.

It is both salutary and satisfying to consider that the genetic conservation of domestic livestock has grown in less than three decades from one or two isolated pockets of interest to a powerful global movement. It has spread from the pastures of a small band of devoted owners to the back garden or paddock of anyone who wishes to keep a few sheep or chickens, and from the confines of the aspirations of a few motivated pioneers to the minds of a multitude of people who are aware of the ethical and social relevance of endangered breeds, in addition to their genetic value, and who wish to give their support. We need you all.

Lawrence Alderson
*June 1994*

# ACKNOWLEDGEMENTS

This book is the culmination of more than twenty-five years close involvement with rare breeds of livestock, during which I have made many good friends, not only in Great Britain but also during visits to many other countries, such as Hungary, Italy, Spain, Australia, U.S.A., Canada, Holland, France, South Africa and elsewhere.

Many of the ideas and policies which I have described were evolved during discussions with these friends so that they are truly international, but I must record my special thanks to many members and officers of the Rare Breeds Survival Trust for their interest, encouragement and support.

Many people and organisations have generously provided photographs to augment my own collection, and they are acknowledged individually in the captions. Specific items of information are acknowledged in the bibliography as 'personal communication'.

I am grateful also to Alec Jolly, of A.H. Jolly (Editorial) Ltd for his invaluable help and advice, often at unsociable hours, without which the book would not have been possible. Finally, I appreciate very much the forbearance and understanding of my family for any lack of attention to them while my mind was focused on manuscripts and photographs. Their unreserved support was a continual source of inspiration.

*Lawrence Alderson*

# CHAPTER I

# ENDANGERED
# AND EXTINCT

In 1842, referring to Irish Dun cattle, David Low recorded in *Domesticated Animals of the British Isles* that the 'Polled Irish Breed has long been diminishing in numbers and, from long neglect, will probably in a few years cease to be found. Had attention been directed at an earlier period to its preservation, Ireland might have now possessed a true Dairy Breed, not surpassed by any in the Kingdom.' It was not until 1974, 132 years later, that it was officially declared extinct, but in the meantime a long list of other breeds had also disappeared.

The irretrievable loss of species and breeds goes back beyond 1627, when the last Aurochs, the wild ancestor of our domestic cattle, was killed in Jaktorowka Forest in Poland. It has continued unabated ever since, with a special flourish in the United Kingdom in the early 1970s. The only remaining Lincolnshire Curly Coat pigs were sent for slaughter in 1972 after being used in experiments; the last pure-bred Norfolk Horn ram was accidentally drowned in 1973; and the last rites were read over the Irish Dun cattle in 1974. It is difficult to believe that this could happen in the midst of a conservation-oriented society.

We pride ourselves on the progress that we have achieved in many spheres of science and technology, not least in genetics and animal breeding, but our concept of progress urgently needs to be re-examined. Progress towards ill-conceived objectives has resulted in the disappearance of many such valuable breeds. As efficiency of selection increases, change becomes more rapid and the opportunity for loss proportionately greater. Thus the dramatic technological advances of artificial insemination, embryo transfer and genetic engineering, can easily become counter-productive unless carefully controlled and constructively employed. There is a constant danger that selection may be geared exclusively to commercial expediency and may discriminate against characteristics which might be of immeasurable value in the future.

In western Europe more than one third of the breeds of cattle which existed at the beginning of the twentieth century are now extinct, more than 40 per cent are seriously endangered, and half of the remainder are local and vulnerable breeds. In the British Isles alone, at least twenty-six breeds of large domestic livestock have become extinct during this century: each representing an irretrievable loss of genetic material. Among cattle, apart from the Irish Dun we have lost the Alderney, Suffolk Dun, Sheeted Somerset, Blue Albion, Castlemartin, Glamorgan and Caithness; among sheep, the Limestone, St Rona's Hill, Cladagh, Roscommon and Rhiw; among pigs, the Ulster White, Small White, Oxford Sandy and Black, Yorkshire Blue and White, Dorset Gold Tip, Lincolnshire Curly Coat and Cumberland; among horses and ponies, the Manx, Cushendale, Tiree, Long Mynd, Galloway and Goonhilly. The last losses were particularly unnecessary because the founders of the National Pony Society in Britain arbitrarily recognised some breeds, and ignored others which became extinct.

The loss of some breeds seem especially tragic. If the Suffolk Dun had survived, it might have had a great impact on today's dairy industry – even 150 years ago the 'cows of Suffolk though subjected to careless treatment, and supported on the most common kinds of food, are scarcely surpassed by any other in their power of yielding abundant milk'. The Limestone sheep, otherwise known as the Silverdale or Farleton Crag, was a unique hill breed, combining hardiness with a high wool quality and an ability to give birth at different times of the year in a way that no modern hill breed can do. The Lincolnshire Curly Coat was a robust, outdoor pig, with a coat of long white hair quite unlike that of any other British breed, and equalled only by the Mangalitza pig of eastern Europe. It fell foul of the whims of fashion, in no way deserving the cruel succession of events that led to its extinction.

In contrast, the Alderney was just one of three related dairy breeds from the Channel Islands, and as long as the Guernsey and Jersey survive maybe its loss is not so significant, except for sentimental reasons. Similarly, the St Rona's Hill was a distinctive all-white, multihorned breed of sheep whose appeal was strictly aesthetic and transitory. The early demise of the Dorset Gold Tip was brought about by specialised development of its early maturing qualities: pigs of this breed were forced to such high weights that their extreme obesity must have made life an uncomfortable burden. To prevent accidents from suffocation, pillows made of round pieces of wood were placed

ABOVE LEFT:
*Extinct: Suffolk Dun cattle, from which the modern Red Poll breed was developed by crossing with the Red Norfolk*

ABOVE:
*Extinct: St Rona's Hill ram. This breed was related to other multi-horned breeds, such as the Hebridean and Manx Loghtan*

under their snouts when they were recumbent; the effort they needed to walk out of their pens was often so great that the attempt was abandoned. However, while understandably lamenting the loss of the Suffolk Dun, the Limestone, and the Lincolnshire Curly Coat, we should not assume that the Alderney, the St Rona's Hill and the Dorset Gold Tip were not equally the possessors of qualities which, although undetected or irrelevant in the past, might have served some vital purpose in the future.

Many of the breeds which still survive are in serious danger. Farming is as susceptible to fashion as the motor trade – old models are cast aside with a reckless disregard for their true value. If a few breeds can generate a sufficient impetus, with their entrance acclaimed by the fashion writers of the livestock industry, they can expand numerically and geographically far beyond the limits which their inherent qualities can justify. Imported breeds frequently replace native breeds for speculative financial motives rather than for their genetic merit.

In Britain, the Longhorn enjoyed universal admiration in the eighteenth century before it was almost completely superseded by the Shorthorn. However, the phenomenon among dairy breeds in the twentieth century is the Holstein–Friesian. In the early stages of its invasion of Great Britain it enjoyed the benefit of astute and influential patrons so that it spread not only to the fertile lowlands, which were its true habitat, but also to many less favourable locations, purely because it was in vogue. Conditions and situations change, and although there may have been no reason to dispute the right of the Friesian to usurp the long-established dominance of the Shorthorn in Great Britain or of the Normande in France, there is every reason to question the wisdom of breeders who introduced the Friesian into the Shetland Islands in 1923 or, more recently, into the oil-rich countries of the Middle East. The same arguments apply to other species, particularly to pigs whose high reproductive rate and short breeding life make them subject to rapid fluctuations in population size, so that a breed can very quickly become extinct if fashion, misfortune or ill-conceived objectives conspire against it.

In 1974 a survey carried out in Great Britain of domestic breeds of livestock identified forty-eight breeds of cattle, sheep, goats, pigs and horses – about half the total number remaining – that needed help to ensure their survival. By 1991 the situation had improved a little but forty-four breeds still were endangered.

ABOVE:
*Rove goat from the Camargue photographed in 1971*

ABOVE RIGHT:
*Extinct: Rhiw sheep; the last flock owned by E.E. Williams on the Rhiw mountain near Abersoch in Gwynedd in 1954*

They are not breeds that can be dismissed as irrelevant, although they have been brutally described as 'the waste products of the process of domestication', a view that ignores all but short-term standards of evaluation. A more responsible attitude would take account of new concepts and allow for changing requirements in the future. There are other considerations that should not be sacrificed in the interest of the maximum immediate profit: those of sentiment, aesthetic pleasure, or concern for the symbols of tradition and heritage. Breeds that are not currently favoured may yet contribute to the quality of life.

A survey was also carried out in France with equally depressing results: there, even more breeds were in acute danger.

*Endangered Breeds of Livestock in France, 1974*

| | |
|---|---|
| Cattle | Bordelaise, Lourdaise, Aure et Saint-Girons, Mézenc, Ferrandaise, Bressanne, Femeline, Villard-de-Lans, Vosgienne, Froment du Léon, Armoricaine, Flamande, Bretonne Pie Noire, Parthenaise, Bazadaise, Gasconne, Blonde des Pyrénées, Corse, Aubrac, Abondance, Tarentaise, Camargue. |
| Sheep | Camares, Ruthenoise, Larzae, Lauraguaise, Corbière, Caussenarde de Lozère, Cevenole, Sahune, Savournon, Quint, Commune des Alpes, Trieves, d'Ardes, Boulonaise, Cauchoise, Trun, Landaise, Franconie, Morvandelle, Deux, Merinos de Rambouillet, Solognote, d'Ouessant, Rouge de Rossillon, Aure et Campan, Lourdaise, Castillonnaise, Caussenarde des Garrigues, Brigasque, Péone, Thones et Marthod, Bizet, Noire du Velay, Rava, Grivette, Berrichon de l'Indre. |
| Pigs | Corse, Bayeux, Limousin, Gascon, Améliore de l'Est, de Mielan, Pie Noire du Pays, Basque, Cazères. |
| Goats | Corse, Pyrénéen, Rove, Sundgau. |
| Horses | Merens, Camargue, Normande (cob), Pottok pony. |

By 1991 the position was still critical and several breeds of cattle such as Armoricaine (19), Maraichine (32), Lourdaise (38), Froment du Leon (48), Nantaise (56), Bearnaise (74) and Auroise (86) had less than one hundred breeding cows.

Italy also has a large number of endangered breeds. In 1991 breeds of cattle with less than 100 breeding cows were the Cinisara (Sicilia), the Garfagnina (Toscana), the Pontremolese (Toscana), the Grigia Val d'Agiga (Veneto), the Mucca Pisana (Toscana), the Calvana (Toscana) and the Pustertaler Sprinzen (Alto Adige).

The growth of concern with genetic conservation in Great Britain in the early 1960s, when small groups of certain endangered livestock breeds were established in Whipsnade Park by the Zoological Society of London. In 1966 the Food and Agriculture organisation of the United Nations instituted a series of meetings on breed preservation, and in 1968 the Biosphere Conference in Paris formally recommended that domestic animals should be preserved, so that 'the rich variety of their genes will not be forever lost because of the present tendencies in agriculture and animal husbandry to concentrate on a limited and highly selected array of strains'. In 1972 the Stockholm Conference on the Environment proposed that a catalogue of threatened domestic animals should be compiled: three years later, the FAO published 'A Pilot Study on the Conservation of Animal Genetic Resources'.

Meanwhile, in 1968 the Royal Agricultural Society of England and the Zoological Society of London, under the guidance of Christopher Dadd and Dr Idwal Rowlands, had set up a working party to prepare a programme for saving rare breeds. With the formation of the Rare Breeds Survival Trust in 1973, the working party became the Advisory Committee of the Trust (see Appendix, page 158) and later, with some small changes, its first Council. The movement quickly gathered strength and from 1974 onwards advanced on an international front. A monthly journal, *The Ark,* was first published privately in May of that year by Michael Rosenberg and myself, and flourished under the benevolent editorship of 'Noah'. In November a meeting of the Société d'Ethnozootechnie in Paris assessed the position of minority breeds in France, while the following year a similar meeting in Groningen led to the formation of the Dutch Stichting Zeldzame Huisdierrassen in 1976. In 1975 I undertook a coast-to-coast lecture tour of North America, and in 1977 the American Minor Breed Conservancy was founded. The first World Congress of Genetics Applied to Livestock Production was held in Madrid in 1974, and one of its symposia, 'Conservation of Animal Genetic Resources', was concerned directly with rare breeds of livestock. In 1980 the FAO/

Endangered Breeds of Livestock in Great Britain in 1992

| Species/Breed | Number of Breeding Animals | | Ne | Priority Category |
|---|---|---|---|---|
| | Male | Female | | |
| HORSES: | | | | |
| Suffolk | 21 | 90 | 68 | Critical |
| Cleveland Bay | 35 | 150 | 114 | Critical |
| Exmoor Pony | 43 | 160 | 136 | Critical |
| Dales Pony | 54 | 549 | 197 | Vulnerable |
| Irish Draught | 57 | 795 | 213 | At Risk |
| Clydesdale | 80 | 800 | 291 | At Risk |
| Fell Pony | | | | Minority |
| Shire | | | | Minority |
| CATTLE: | | | | |
| Vaynol | 6 | 17 | 18 | Critical |
| Irish Moiled | 16 | 74 | 53 | Critical |
| Shetland | 18e | 150e | 64e | Critical |
| Kerry | 21e | 274e | 78e | Critical |
| White Park | 24 | 250 | 88 | Endangered |
| Gloucester | 44 | 350 | 156 | Vunerable |
| Beef Shorthorn | 54 | 590 | 198 | Vunerable |
| Red Poll | 68 | 973 | 254 | Vunerable |
| British White | 83 | 730 | 298 | At Risk |
| Longhorn | | | | Minority |
| Dexter | | | | Minority |
| Belted Galloway | | | | Minority |
| Devon | | | | Watching |
| Lincoln Red | | | | Watching |
| Chillingham | | | | Feral |
| SHEEP: | | | | |
| Castlemilk Moorit | 19 | 169 | 68 | Critical |
| Norfolk Horn | 39 | 329 | 139 | Critical |
| Portland | 85 | 744 | 305 | Endangered |
| North Ronaldsay | 162 | 984 | 556 | Endangered |
| Leicester Longwool | 105 | 692 | 365 | Endangered |
| Whitefaced Woodland # | 35 | 387 | 128 | Vunerable |
| Manx Loghtan | 55 | 708 | 204 | Vunerable |
| Soay * | 88 | 436 | 293 | Vunerable |
| Cotswold | 73 | 928 | 270 | Vunerable |
| Wensleydale | 93 | 562 | 319 | Vunerable |
| Hebridean | 77 | 821 | 282 | Vunerable |
| Hill Radnor # | 54e | 1149 | 206 | Vunerable |
| Greyface Dartmoor | 147 | 1186 | 523 | At Risk |
| Lincoln Longwool | 114 | 1467 | 423 | At Risk |
| Wiltshire Horn | 115 | 1600 | 429 | At Risk |
| Southdown | 120 | 1850 | 451 | At Risk |
| Shropshire | 119 | 1871 | 448 | At Risk |
| Ryeland | | | | At Risk |
| Teeswater | | | | At Risk |
| Oxford Down | | | | Minority |
| Shetland | | | | Minority |
| Whitefaced Dartmoor | | | | Watching |
| Dorset Down | | | | Watching |
| South Welsh Mountain | | | | Watching |
| Devon & Cornwall Longwool | | | | Watching |
| Boreray | | | | Feral |
| PIGS: | | | | |
| Tamworth | 48 | 127 | 139 | Critical |
| British Lop | 44 | 184 | 142 | Critical |
| Middle White | 50 | 154 | 151 | Critical |
| Large Black | 34 | 254 | 120 | Critical |
| Berkshire | 80 | 271 | 247 | Endangered |
| British Saddleback | 92 | 441 | 310 | Endangered |
| GOS | 68 | 417 | 234 | Endangered |
| GOATS: | | | | |
| Bagot | 19e | 87e | 62e | Critical |
| Golden Guernsey | 49 | 236 | 162 | At Risk |

# Large unregistered population    e Estimated    * Large feral population

UNEP Technical Consultation on Animal Genetic Resources Conservation and Management in Rome brought together expert delegates from all parts of the world.

*The last pure-bred Garfagnina cow, at 24 years of age, found by the author in the hills north of Lucca during a visit to Tuscany in 1980*

The development of private, non-governmental organisations (NGOs) for rare breeds began in 1969 with the creation in the U.K. of an informal group which was formalised as the Rare Breeds Survival Trust in 1973. This example was followed, slowly at first, by Stichting Zeldzame Huisdierrassen in the Netherlands (1976) and the American Minor Breeds Conservancy in the USA (1977), then with an accelerating tempo by Gesellschaft zur Erhaltung alter und gefahrdeter Haustierrassen in Germany (1981), Pro Specie Rara in Switzerland (1982), Joywind Farm Conservancy in Canada (1986), Rare Breeds Conservancy in New Zealand, Sociedad Espanola pro Recursos Geneticos Animales in Spain and Vereniging voor het Behoud van Zeldzame Huisdierrassen in Belgium in 1989, the Australian Rare Breeds Reserve and IDAAM in Greece in 1990, and the Institute for Agricultural Biodiversity in the USA in 1991.

This rapid growth and the global representation led to the realisation of the need for an international organisation to co-ordinate national and regional activities, and an international conference convened by the Rare Breeds Survival Trust in 1989 appointed an Organising Committee and

*Rossa Pontremolese cow. A triple-purpose breed noted for its thriftiness, hardiness and the richness of its milk; the cows are light red in colour and the skin is strongly pigmented; there is a mealy coloured ring around the muzzle. The growth rings on the horns of this cow indicate her great age of 23 years. Italy shares with France and Great Britain particularly rich genetic resources in her cattle breeds. In 1947 there were 42 Italian breeds of cattle; by 1974 only 22 breeds remained, and of these 13 were gravely endangered*

charged it with this responsibility. As a result, Rare Breeds International (RBI) was registered with charitable status and incorporated in 1991. It held its first Congress in Budapest in August of that year, and in 1992 combined its annual meeting in Cordoba with the quincentenary celebrations of Columbus' first voyage to the Americas. The author was elected founder chairman of RBI, with Professor Roy Crawford of the University of Saskatchewan as vice-chairman.

All the private national organisations are associated with RBI, which also enjoys the support of 'hybrid' organisations in other countries where state and private programmes are combined. These broader based programmes have developed in Italy, Austria, France, Brazil and the Scandinavian countries. Many other countries, particularly in Africa and Asia, have relied on state programmes with less ambitious objectives. However, this generalisation does not always hold true; Hungary has long-established state conservation programmes of support for breeds such as Grey Steppe cattle, Mangalitza pigs, Zackel sheep and Nonius horses.

RBI is in the early stages of development, but it has identified and detailed its programme of activities and defined its role in the global context. It complements the work of other organisations such as the World Association of Animal Production, the United Nations Environment Programme and the Food and Agriculture Organisation of the United Nations which co-ordinates governmental programmes.

An important function of RBI is to monitor the status of 'multinational' breeds. For example, although the Lincoln Longwool sheep is an endangered breed in its country of origin, it was exported in 1862 to Argentina, where more than 10,000 animals of the breed were registered in 1986, and where there are now more then 100 pedigree flocks. The global population of the Lincoln Longwool, and other breeds such as the Tamworth pig and Red Poll cattle, is a better indicator of their endangered status than the founder population in the country of origin.

The survey of 'multinational' breeds leads RBI to a study of the relationship between breeds, a factor which can help to identify the most efficient methods of conservation. An analysis of the genetic distance of the different breeds in the Zaupel group of sheep in the Danubian countries would indicate whether it would be more appropriate to conserve them as one breed, or to maintain them as the four existing separate breeds. Similar studies could be made of Criollo cattle and

*Fribourgeois cow from Switzerland; she weighed 613.6 kg in 1972 at 14 years of age*

BELOW LEFT:
*The last pure-bred Fribourgeois bull, Heron, in 1972 at 2½ years of age*

of the feral descendants of the Andalusian horse in America.

The dissemination of information is another prime function of RBI, through media which vary from newsletters to international conferences. It is also concerned to undertake conservation projects in parts of the world where a national or regional organisation does not exist, but the current trends indicate that the majority of countries will have established a programme for genetic conservation in the near future.

The position of rare breeds varies from country to country, and where the situation is serious the main burden of blame often rests on the shoulders of government departments. In Norway, the

*Svana (Swan), a 30-year old Vestland Fjordfe cow in Norway. Isolated pockets of endangered Norwegian breeds have survived despite earlier Government policy*

Institute of Animal Breeding at Vollebekk established a national breeding programme which, in the name of progress, effectively eliminated all breeds of Norwegian cattle except one. It is true that in 1959 only 32 per cent of the national dairy herd in Norway was recorded for milk production, showing an average lactation yield of 150 kg butter-fat, while the average yield had risen to 195 kg butter-fat in 1971 with 58 per cent of the cows being recorded, but the cost of this achievement was a terrible loss of native breeds, and the validity of butterfat production as a measure of value is already under question.

At the beginning of this century Norway possessed about twenty breeds of cattle. By 1959 only seven recognised breeds remained, with the NRF (Norsk Rodtfe) making up about 30 per cent of the national herd. This breed was then chosen as the medium for implementing government breeding policies, and breeders were encouraged and advised to use NRF bulls. The result is that 98 per cent of the cattle in Norway are now of NRF type. It is frightening to consider both the speed of this process and the overwhelming effect of an imposed policy with government support. In the 1960s a series of breeds were carried away in the torrent of amalgamation with the NRF – the Rodt Tronderfe in 1960, the Raukolle in 1961, the Dole in 1963, and the SVF (Sor og Vestlandsfe) in 1968. In 1984 a Nordic Gene Bank Committee was formed to co-ordinate genetic conservation programmes throughout Scandinavia, and small numbers of these near-extinct breeds have been found on remote farms and it is hoped that they can be saved as pure-breeding populations.

In Holland, early this century, government livestock officers actively discouraged the minor breeds, such as the Witrik, the Lakenvelder and the Blaarkop, and their Herd Book was closed in 1932. Thus in 1950, when bull-licensing regulations forbidding the keeping of bulls not registered with the Dutch Herd Book Society came into force, these breeds were deprived of bulls for pure breeding. Thus they are effectively extinct and remain only as names linked to particular colour patterns.

In Germany, government officials have controlled breed registration programmes and have tended to ignore a breed when the population falls below one hundred animals, thus allowing it to become extinct by default.

In eastern Europe the situation is different. For example, Hungary possesses important genetic material in breeds such as the Grey Steppe cattle, the Zackel sheep and the Mangalitza pig, and has established policies to conserve these breeds. More recently Hungary has taken the initiative in

LEFT:
*Witrik cow. This breed was noted for its high yield of milk, and its decline was due to political pressure rather than a lack of genetic quality*

BELOW LEFT:
*Lakenvelder cow. The belted pattern in cattle, found also in the Belted Galloway, Dutch Belted and Bolian Gwynion, as well as the extinct Sheeted Somerset, seems to have originated in Holland*

organising international training seminars in Budapest for genetic conservation programmes. The position in some neighbouring countries is less encouraging. The upheavals caused by the overthrow of the old regimes in 1989, and the outbreak of hostilities in some areas, has placed endangered breeds at even greater risk in eastern Europe and throughout the old Soviet Union.

In Great Britain the official attitude to the conservation of rare breeds has been strictly neutral, but organisations such as the Milk Marketing Board have given valuable support, and the Rare Breeds Survival Trust, as a private organisation unfettered by bureaucratic protocol, has made great progress, not only in Britain but also in assisting other groups in Europe and North America. In fairness it must be recorded that the British government ordered the shipment of a group of White

RIGHT:
*Grey Steppe bull in Hungary in 1983*

BELOW RIGHT:
*Mangalitza sow in Hungary in 1983*

Park cattle to North America in 1940 to safeguard a precious national heritage if the United Kingdom were invaded. This herd was preserved on the King Ranch in Texas and is now in Iowa. There is also close co-operation between the Trust and the livestock departments of the Ministry of Agriculture, Fisheries and Food. Throughout the European Community there is an increasing awareness of the importance of the genetic conservation of domestic livestock and in 1991 the European Parliament approved special incentive payments for endangered breeds.

The position in the Americas is unusual, as most American domestic livestock is descended from imported ancestors and there are few genuinely native breeds. Yet as long ago as 1927 the Federal Government took positive action to save the Texas Longhorn by financing the creation of two herds in Oklahoma and Nebraska. The Texas Longhorn is derived from imported Spanish cattle –

ABOVE LEFT:
*A Canadienne bull. An attempt to save this
breed has been made by crossing with the
Brown Swiss*

ABOVE:
*A Dutch Belted cow in the Barrett herd in
Massachusettes in 1975*

LEFT:
*Devon cattle ploughing in New England
where the original type of the breed has been
maintained*

the original type can be closely identified in the Andalucian breeds – but it is so closely associated with the romantic history of the cattle trails and pioneering of the Wild West that it is accepted as an American breed. The Criollo breeds of cattle and sheep in Latin America, as well as special groups in North America such as Florida Cracker cattle, Ossabaw Island pigs and some feral horses, are descended from Iberian stock which first arrived in the Americas 500 years ago.

Surveys in North America list about forty endangered breeds of large farm livestock, of which twenty-three were derived from British stock. Two breeds of cattle which have their origin in continental Europe are the Dutch Belted and the Canadienne. The Dutch Belted is descended from Lakenvelder cattle first imported from Holland by Barney Barnum in 1838, but is now closer to the original type than the modern Lakenvelder. The Canadienne is descended from an extinct breed that was found formerly in Brittany. Thus North America has become a repository of valuable

*Arapawa feral sheep from New Zealand carry white marks which show the influence of the 'spotting' gene*

genes, and the quickening interest has been stimulated partly by the romance of the Texas Longhorn and partly by the development of living historical farms such as Colonial Williamsburg in Virginia and Old Sturbridge Village in Massachusetts. At centres such as these, searches have been made for authentic old types of livestock that were imported in the early days of European colonisation. In New England projects have been established to identify and preserve Milking Devon cattle and 'lineback' Witrik types, often using old records of stray animals as a source of information.

In New Zealand the development of the stock imported in the early days of exploration has followed a different course. Feral populations have existed since the earliest times of settlement when domestic stock, much of it from England, was allowed to roam in unfenced country or was deliberately turned free. Feral cattle are based mainly on Shorthorn stock and are limited in numbers, but the populations of both goats and pigs are widespread. Both species were introduced as early as the 1770s by Captain Cook, and a reversion to ancestral type has been noted especially among the feral pigs, where some piglets are born with stripes along the body as in wild boar piglets. There are several self-maintaining groups of feral sheep on the mainland and on islands. They are derived mainly from Merino stock, but the feral flock on Arapawa Island shows how much the characteristics of a population can change in less than a century. For example, 90 per cent of the Arapawa flock is more or less black, and the fleece is shed annually. There are also small populations of rare breeds of British sheep in New Zealand, namely Lincoln Longwool, Leicester Longwool, Shropshire and Ryeland, and these may provide an opportunity to replenish the blood lines in Great Britain by an exchange of stock. Similarly four rare pig breeds of British origin, namely the Berkshire, Large Black, Saddleback and Tamworth, have been or are about to be re-imported to the United Kingdom from Australia.

*Chillingham cattle. Mature bulls weigh about 300 kg, and cows about 280 kg with a withers height of 110 cm. A domesticated White Park cow weighs about 637 kg and stands 130.5 cm at the withers*

The loss of breeds has been greatest in countries with highly developed, intensive livestock industries employing advanced breeding techniques. In undeveloped countries, where their position usually appears less serious, there is a real danger that the impact of modern technology on nomadic and peasant communities will quickly imperil native breeds. This applies to derived breeds such as the Criollo of southern and central America, but is even more important in the case of the native breeds of Africa. The demand for western technology in the developing world, especially when it is exploited by the use of semen or embryos from high performance breeds, has already threatened the survival of some native breeds. There is concern for the future of breeds such as the heat-tolerant Sahiwal which is the best indigenous dairy breed in India and Pakistan; the Hu sheep in China, which is prolific throughout a long breeding season; and the Sayoumi chicken in Egypt which is a remarkable laying bird whose ancestors were known to the Pharaohs. Those who advocate the use of exotic breeds in the developing world take insufficient account of the quality of the

*Berrenda en Negra cow grazing sparse summer pasture in the dehesa in Andalucia. This breed formed part of the ancestral stock of the Criollo cattle of the Americas*

feed resources, climate, the standard of management and the prevelant parasites and disease. The value of retaining native types that are efficiently adapted to their environment is vividly illustrated by the Kuri cattle of Lake Chad. In a 1975 FAO report on these cattle Ian Mason defined their qualities:

> The humpless Kuri breed of Lake Chad is unique in its habitat and morphology. Its inflated spongy horns are unknown in any other breed. Its habitat is, for cattle, a very special one, namely the islands and shores of Lake Chad. To this environment it is remarkably adapted and animals are able to subsist on the coarse forage of the shores and to swim from island to island to reach new pasture. The Kuri is a moderate milker and an excellent beef animal… There is no doubt that the Kuri has a great potential as a meat producer. It is clearly well adapted to its natural environment and the breeding herd appears to flourish on natural pastures. At the same time the males appear to respond well to feedlot fattening. Their docility is truly amazing.

The majority of Kuri cattle are white with black points and large, lyre-shaped horns, but a proportion have the characteristic buoy-shaped, inflated horns which are a distinctive feature of the breed. The animals swim with their heads tilted back so that the horns lie on the surface of the water; this increases their buoyancy and so improves their mobility in the water. In the last twenty or thirty years, the reduction of the grazing area and crossing with the humped Zebu cattle have reduced the numbers and endangered the purity of the Kuri.

Throughout the world there remains an enormous fund of genetic resources in the minority breeds which must be saved from further tragic depletion. If the initial impetus created by the FAO and the Rare Breeds Survival Trust can be maintained, there is a chance that the list of extinct domestic breeds will grow no larger.

# CHAPTER 2

# THE ORIGIN
# OF BREEDS

*Clydesdales ploughing at Loweswater in the Lake District in the mid-1930s*

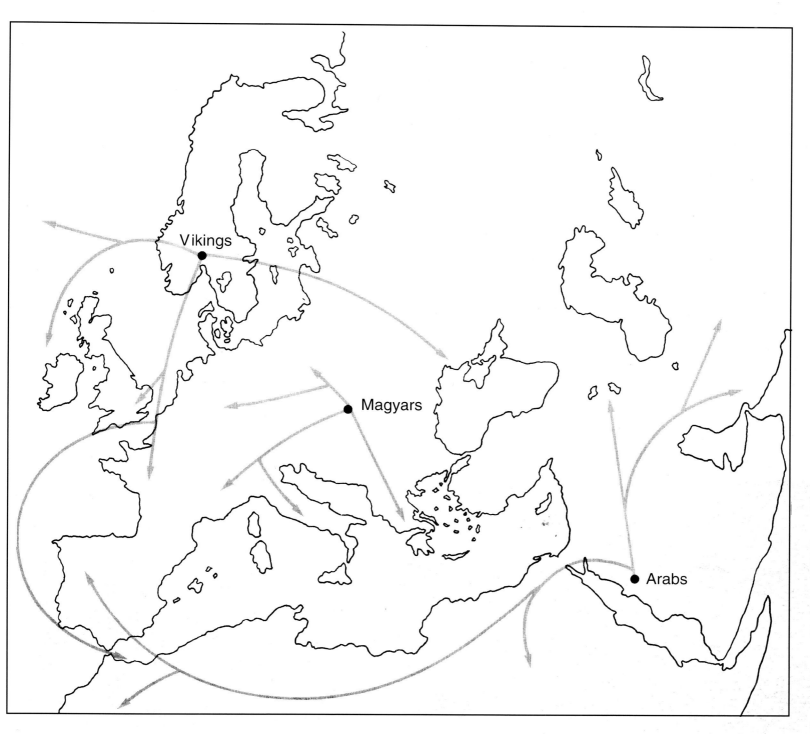

Vikings

Magyars

Arabs

*Movement of Peoples in the First Millennium AD: The first millennium AD saw particularly violent displacement and migration of tribes and whole populations throughout Europe and North Africa, and it was during this period that different types of livestock from widely separated regions were mixed so thoroughly that the ancestry of modern breeds is always likely to remain a partial mystery. There had been some movements of livestock during the first millennium BC, but they were of less importance. The seafaring Phoenicians had introduced new breeds of dog to Britain while trading with the tin mines in Cornwall, the Celts played a small part in the transfer of some Germanic cattle, while the Romans brought polled, whitefaced sheep to Britain*

## Migrations and Conquests

More than 10,000 years ago, the Neolithic revolution brought settled agriculture to the valleys of the Tigris and Euphrates. The hunters of the Paleolithic period gradually settled down during the Mesolithic transition and became the owners of domesticated livestock. These changes did not occur everywhere at the same time; the Baltic peoples were 5000 years behind the advanced culture of Mesopotamia in developing stable agricultural systems.

Some early Mesopotamian cities were in the extreme south of the country, on the shores of the Persian Gulf, on land which had not long been formed by the silting up of the Tigris and Euphrates. Most species of farm livestock were first domesticated in this area, and the early improvements in breeding were recorded here. In Mesopotamia as early as the third millennium BC cattle were fed grain during much of the year for beef production, a dairy industry manufactured butter and cheese, and draught oxen pulled ploughs and carts. The inventory of an estate near Lagash in southern Mesopotamia included a bull imported from the upland kingdom of Elam to prevent deterioration of the herd in the sultry climate of the plain.

From the areas of advanced agriculture where they were domesticated it is likely that the improved strains of livestock were spread mainly by nomadic tribes and by military conquest. As early as the fourth millennium BC the ancient Sumerian civilisation in the Middle East was extending its influence peacefully and interchanging livestock and goods with the Indian civilisations, but the first important phase of activity started around 3000 BC in two main centres. On the one hand, the peoples inhabiting the area between Mesopotamia and Egypt known as the Fertile Crescent were spreading gradually with a variety of livestock in four directions: eastwards to India; westward along the northern shores of Africa to the Iberian Peninsula; north-westwards through Anatolia, along the valley of the Danube and on to Scandinavia; and finally across the Mediterranean and western Europe to Britain. In contrast, at about the same time, a warlike and nomadic people emerged from the southern Steppes of Russia and fanned out in a widespread migration, penetrating into both India and central Europe; they were skilful horsemen who took livestock with them.

The next major movement of peoples occurred mainly during the late third millennium BC and the second millennium BC. The main invasion of the Steppe people into central Europe turned southwards and swept down into the Mediterranean basin in the three distinct waves of the Ionians, the Achaeans, and finally the Dorians. A subsidiary branch (the Battle-Axe people) continued westwards, reaching Scandinavia and the north-western shores of Europe. Meanwhile, the inhabitants of Egypt and northern Africa were pressing southwards down both sides of the continent, and the Iberians or Beaker people spread throughout western Europe and Britain. The Beaker people reached Britain around 1900 BC, when the pyramids of Egypt had already been built for a thousand years, Agamemnon was about to lead the Achaeans against Troy, and Abraham was still living in Mesopotamia.

Although the Celts began to arrive in Britain around 750 BC, about two centuries after the reign of Solomon and at roughly the same time as the first Olympic games in 776, the third major phase of activity in the spread of livestock did not occur until more than a thousand years later. In the seventh century AD, the sudden eruption of Islamic fervour swept through northern Africa into Spain and encircled the Sahara, where the influence of the Islamic peoples' hot-blooded horses can be seen in the modern breeds. Two centuries later, in central Europe, the Magyars, displaced from their own homeland, were wreaking havoc in Germany, France, and particularly in Italy. Further north, the Scandinavian explosion was motivated by the pressures of an increasing population, and their skill as sailors enabled the Vikings to colonise most of the western seaboard of Europe.

The ancestry and present location of modern livestock breeds can be traced in the patterns of these tribal migrations and military conquests. The nomadic tribes played an important role, as they were pastoralists who took their livestock with them. They were also horsemen, and the horse was the basis of their success. It is unlikely that accurate details of the origin and development of our modern breeds will ever be discovered, but it is possible to construct an impressionistic view which conveys the general hypothesis, although the details may be indistinct. Apart from the value of historical documents and the movements of human populations the evidence may be sought in archaeology, circumstantial evidence, genetic fingerprinting, osteology, and the visual characteristics of each breed.

## Horses

Unlike other livestock, the horse was originally domesticated during the late Neolithic period by the warlike inhabitants of the Steppes rather than in the settled agriculture of the Fertile Crescent. However, wild horses and ponies were domesticated independently in different parts of the world,

*Exmoor Ponies in their native habitat*

and whereas cattle are probably derived from a single wild ancestor, the origins of the horse can be traced to four distinct sub-species. There is still considerable controversy on this point, but the theories of Hermann Ebhardt, a German horse breeder, based on observations of the behaviour of different breeds, are confirmed by much of the evidence obtained from archaeological sources. Genetic distance studies have demonstrated that the relationship between modern breeds supports this hypothesis. There are five main groups, namely the ponies (which need to be analysed further), the heavy draught breeds, the Thoroughbred group, the Arab group and the breeds descended from the Andalucian which itself was derived largely from Barb ancestry.

Of the four ancestral species or types which Ebhardt identified, the first is the Northern pony which existed in Alaska at least 100,000 years ago, and is now represented in its three phases by the Exmoor Pony, the Konik of Poland, and Przewalski's horse, which are adapted respectively to tundra and similar ecosystems, to the forests of Europe, and to the steppes of central Asia. Bones

comparable to those of the Exmoor Pony have been found in caves in the Mendip Hills, close to the breed's present home, at levels dating from 60,000 BC, and also in Alaska from an even earlier period. This type originated in the East and emigrated westwards during the Ice Age, reaching western Europe via the Balkans and Spain.

The Exmoor Pony has the primitive equine colouring of dun with an overcoat of dark brown, but this merges into a lighter mealy colour under the belly and inside the forearms and thighs. The mealy nose is a distinctive point of the breed, as is the mealy coloration around the eyes ('cingle') and the pronounced eyebrow known as 'toad eye'. The breed has an unusual primitive blood type that is dissimilar to that of the Thoroughbred and Arab. Mares should not exceed 12.2 hands or stallions 12.3 hands high (1 hand = 4 in or 10 cm). The forehead is wide, the nostrils are broad, and the ears short and thick. The legs are clean and short with good bone. There is a small tuft of hair on the fetlocks, and the ergots and chestnuts are very small, or may be absent. The forelimbs are constructed to give the animal perfect balance while subjecting the fetlock and suspensory ligaments to the least possible strain.

The Exmoor Pony is more capable than red deer or mountain sheep of living outdoors through-

TOP LEFT:
*A Highland Pony mare and foal*

TOP RIGHT:
*Ardennais horse: the oldest of the heavy breeds*

ABOVE LEFT:
*A Caspian mare, Taliyeh, from Iran, and her foal, Banafsheh*

ABOVE RIGHT:
*The Old English Black Horse: a stallion bred in Derbyshire in the early nineteenth century, from a painting by William Shiels, R.S.A.*

*A group of White Park cattle, owned by the Royal Agricultural Society of England, in Stoneleigh Park in Warwickshire*

out the year on a meagre diet of roughage. Its hardiness is due to the extent to which it has retained the distinctive characteristics of the prototype. In its roomy nasal cavity the large turbinate bones can provide the greatest possible surface area to warm the intake of air. The jaw provides implantation for large, strong teeth which can make the fullest use of poor grazing. Protection against harsh weather is provided mainly by the strong, wiry hairs of the outer coat, which sheds the rain and keeps dry such vital and sensitive areas as the dock, inguinal region and the belly, thus reducing loss of body heat. It is remarkable how the Exmoor Pony keeps its flesh and spirit on small quantities of feed under difficult conditions.

Type 2, the Northern Great Horse, is larger than the Northern pony. It also migrated westwards, but at a later date and by a more northerly route – through the gap between the ice caps of the Alps and Scandinavia when the ice had retreated. It is represented by the Merens horse in the Pyrenees, and by the Fell and Highland ponies in Great Britain, all of them much smaller than their huge ancestor of the last interglacial period, which stood as much as 18 hands high. The Highland Pony was the native breed of Scotland from the Outer Hebrides to Perthshire, and different types developed as a result of the varying conditions between the islands and the mainland. The small island ponies from the Hebrides are maybe two hands shorter than the Garron type found on the mainland which may stand up to 15 hands high. The most common colour is dun with a black dorsal stripe. The Highland Pony has a deep chest and powerful quarters and loins, which enable it to carry great weights on the steep slopes of the Scottish Highlands, but previously it was considered inferior to the now extinct Galloway. These ponies are used by sportsmen to carry heavy loads of deer weighing up to 115 kg from the hill walks and forests.

Type 3, *Equus mosbachensis,* can trace back its ancestry to the large horse of the Middle Pleistocene period and was apparently always restricted to Europe. Its relatively small teeth were adapted to the marsh and woodland grazing of the Rhine valley. A non-migratory type, it was the ancestor of the heavy breeds of draught horse, most of which were derived from the ancient Ardennes breed. The modern Belgian or Brabançon is a direct descendant of the Ardennes, while another offshoot, the Flemish, exerted a profound influence on the development of the British heavy-horse breeds, especially the Shire and the Clydesdale.

Type 4 shows some affinity to the Northern pony, but was a fundamentally different animal, more delicate and finely constructed, like its present-day descendant, the Arab. It developed in a subtropical climate with high rainfall, and browsed rather than grazed. Its best modern representative is the Caspian, which was rediscovered in Iran in 1965. In contrast to the Exmoor Pony, the Caspian horse, although standing only 10.3 to 12.3 hands high, is slender and finely-drawn. The head is short with a small muzzle and a shallow jaw, and its narrow conformation is that of a small Thoroughbred or Arab. Its narrow, hard, oval-shaped hooves confirm its ancient status, and horses of a similar height, with the typical vaulted forehead of the Caspian, have been identified on stone carvings at Persepolis from the first millennium BC and on the trilingual seal of Darius the Great of Persia from about the same time.

Most modern breeds are a mixture of these four types, and many were fixed some time ago. The Shetland Pony probably is a mixture of types 1 and 2, but its size has been reduced by both natural and artificial selection in a difficult environment. More recently most of the native British pony breeds have been modified by crossing with the Arab (type 4), with only the Exmoor, Highland, Fell and Dales remaining relatively free of its influence. However, the Dales Pony, originally type 2, has been crossed to some extent with the Clydesdale, itself a mixture of types 2 and 3, so that today it resembles a miniature carthorse. In contrast the Percheron, derived from type 3, has had some introduction of Arab blood which has refined its head and enlivened its action. There are more than 160 recognised breeds of horse and pony in the world, some of which are international breeds.

The horse was a relatively unimportant animal in the most advanced early civilisations and achieved more widespread distribution only when harnessed to the war chariot in the middle of the second millennium BC. It was not until about 1000 BC that the riding of horses was practised widely, although it had been accomplished at least a thousand years earlier by the Bactrians, whose kingdom – perhaps better known as the romantic land of Samarkand – lay on the northern slopes of the Afghan mountain ranges astride the Silk Road to China. They bred the 'blood-sweating, heavenly horses' which were envied by the rulers of China, and valued for their speed as early as 1000 BC. They became the Turkoman (or Turkmene), the most important ancestor of the modern Thoroughbred. The Bactrians, and their Scythian neighbours, exerted a profound influence on many aspects of horse breeding and management throughout the world. Polo is derived from the ancient Bactrian game of baiga; the stirrup was invented by the Scythians; while Viking, Celtic and early Anglo-Saxon art is derived from Scythian art, which revolved around the horse.

## Cattle

Cattle were domesticated much earlier than the horse, probably more than 10,000 years ago. It is likely that all modern breeds are descended from one wild species, *Bos primigenius,* better known as the Urus or Aurochs, and that domestication first took place in the area bounded by the Persian Gulf, the Caspian Sea, the Black Sea and the Mediterranean Sea. *Bos primigenius* was found in Europe, Asia and North Africa between 30° and 60° latitude, and it is significant that many adult people in more southern areas (Africa, eastern Asia, and southern Europe to some extent) are unable to absorb the lactose in fresh milk.

By 4000 BC the Hamitic (humpless) Longhorn was well established as a domesticated type of cattle and was spreading into Africa, while improved types were already being developed. An Egyptian mural relief of the twenty-fifth century BC shows polled and shorthorn cattle with such characteristics as pied coats and large udders.

The longhorned cattle were originally domesticated for religious and sacrificial purposes, while shorthorned cattle were valued more highly as agricultural animals. They too were lyre-horned, but they were hardier and rapidly superseded the longhorned, spreading into Africa and across Europe around 3000 BC. Polled cattle were an accepted feature in herds by 2000 BC. A record from the tomb of the Egyptian prince Me-henwet-Re in the same period shows that he owned 750 donkeys, 974 sheep, 2234 goats, 835 horned and 220 polled cattle, and that the cattle were of many colours. Humped cattle appeared at about the same time and spread into both Africa and India. The initial type, the Longhorn Zebu, was taken down the migration route of the Hottentots as far as the Cape of Good Hope. The Shorthorn Zebu was a much later development and formed the basis of modern Indian breeds. It spread also to central Africa around AD 700–800.

TOP: *An Aurochs from an old print found in an antique shop in Augsburg in 1827. No exact record of the size or colour of the Aurochs remains*

ABOVE: *White Park cattle in Iowa in 1983 after being moved from the King Ranch in Texas*

These four types, Hamitic Longhorn, Hamitic Shorthorn, humped Longhorn and humped Short-horn, are represented by various modern breeds. The Hamitic Longhorn can be seen in the Kuri cattle of Lake Chad, while the cattle of northern Europe show a strong influence of the Shorthorn. There are no pure Longhorn Zebu breeds, but the Sanga (Hamitic Longhorn mixed with Longhorn Zebu) type includes the Fulani, Nguni and Afrikander cattle. The Shorthorn Zebu includes all the Indian breeds and the Boran of East Africa.

In western Europe the picture is more complex and confused, but four main influences can be identified. Cattle from Spain, mainly of Hamitic Longhorn type, which spread over much of west-ern Europe early in the second millennium BC, probably constitute the major influence in the development of such breeds as the White Park, Welsh Black, Camargue, Kerry, Longhorn and Highland, as well as the native Andalucian breeds and their derivatives in the Americas. These animals were the cattle identified in Neolithic sites in Britain. Their horns were wide-spreading, with a forward and upward curve. It is interesting to compare the similarities of such breeds as the N'Dama of West Africa, the Camargue of southern France and the Kerry of Ireland, all found on the old migration route of the Hamitic Longhorn.

The short-horned type began to infiltrate the British Isles during the Iron Age and was later reinforced by the importation of Germanic cattle, mainly red in colour, with medium or short horns. The Angeln is the most typical representative of this group, which also includes the Danish Red, Lincoln Red and other red British beef breeds.

The Magyars were responsible for introducing cattle with medium lyre-shaped horns and a mealy ring around the muzzle to most of southern Europe. The Grey Steppe represents the basic type, while the Brown Swiss, found in the Alpine region, the Limousin, Aubrac, Tarentaise and several other breeds in France, and most of the breeds in northern Italy, northern Spain and Portu-gal, belong to this group. This type may have influenced the Jersey, Guernsey and South Devon, but the haemoglobin B gene carried by these breeds is more likely to have resulted from a direct infusion of blood from Zebu cattle.

The Vikings made an equally strong impact on the development of cattle breeds in north-western Europe. Their cattle showed considerable variation, but it must be remembered that uni-formity within a breed or type had not been established at that time. In addition, Scandinavia had been affected by most of the earlier movements of population – the Danubians, who built the Swiss lake dwellings, the Battle-Axe people, the Beaker folk and the Celts – so that their cattle were of mixed origin. They were polled (Finn cattle) or lyre-horned (Telemark), dun in colour (Dole and Sor-og Vestlandsfe) or white with black points (Fjall). Their influence is evident in the Normande and Breton cattle in France, the Channel Island breeds, the Irish Moiled, and the Shetland, Short-horn and Red Poll (via the extinct Suffolk Dun) in Great Britain.

## Sheep and Goats

There is still considerable speculation as to whether the domestic sheep is descended from only one wild ancestor, the Moufflon *(Ovis musimon)*, or whether it has evolved also from the Asian wild sheep, the Urial *(O. vignei)* and Argali *(O. ammon)*. The 'single source' theory depends on the fact that, of these three wild types, only the Moufflon shares the same diploid chromosome number (54) with domestic sheep, whereas the Argali has 56 and the Urial varies from 54 to 58. However, all types have the same amount of chromosome material, and this is the important factor as it permits the various species to interbreed and produce fertile progeny. There are several characteristics, especially in the shapes of skull and horn, which strongly support the argument for a multiple origin. The perverted horns and the mane on the throat and neck of Urial rams are reflected in the modern North Ronaldsay sheep, and the heavily spiralled horns of the black-faced hill breeds of Britain could find their origin in the imposing heads of the wild Argali sheep.

It is not clear how sheep breeds developed after their domestication some time before 8000 BC,

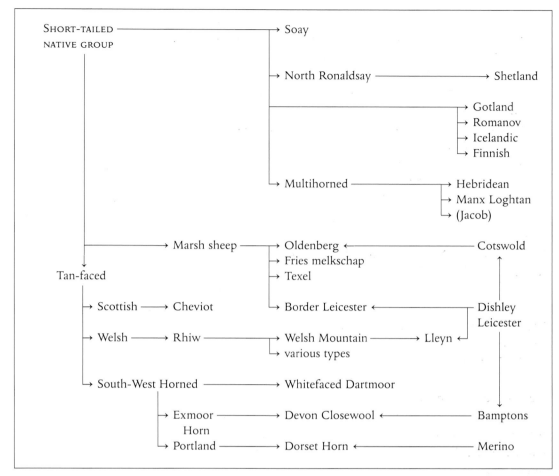

and we cannot pick up the threads until a little over 2500 years ago. At that time Britain was the home of primitive sheep, probably little changed from the original type now represented by the Soay, whereas white wool as fine as that of the modern Merino was already being produced in the area around the Black Sea (which includes Colchis, where Jason found the Golden Fleece). In much of Britain the short-tailed type, which possesses a distinctive scapula with a long, narrow neck as well as the characteristic of tail length, was not replaced by long-tailed sheep until about the fifteenth century. At the beginning of the nineteenth century Culley recorded short-tailed and dun-faced sheep in the Scottish Highlands, and similar sheep still survive on the northern and western fringes of the British Isles.

More recent British breeds seem to have been derived from three sources. The tan-faced, horned primitive sheep, probably established in northern Europe from about 3000 BC, provided the basis from which new breeds were developed. It was related to the Northern Short-tailed group, which includes the North Ronaldsay, Shetland, Icelandic, Spelsau of Norway, Gotland, Finnish and Romanov, and also contributed to the Portland, the extinct Rhiw and the ancestral forms of the Cheviot on mainland Britain. The table shows the main lines of descent, but the Jacob may well be more closely related to Spanish sheep than to the Hebridean group. Breeds such as the Exmoor Horn, Welsh Mountain and Cheviot were also considerably influenced by crossing with white-faced sheep, although the Cheviot was still dun-faced and horned at the end of the eighteenth century.

The white-faced, hornless sheep introduced into Britain mainly during the period of Roman occupation was the first of the imported types whose characteristics were superimposed on native stock in the evolution of most modern British breeds. It diverged into two distinct types, the longwools, of which the Lincoln and the Teeswater are the purest and most ancient representatives, and the medium-shortwools, which played a part in the evolution of the Down breeds. Here again only the main lines of descent are shown. The Merino does not fit neatly into any group of sheep, having been developed separately as a finewool breed in Scythia more than 2000 years ago.

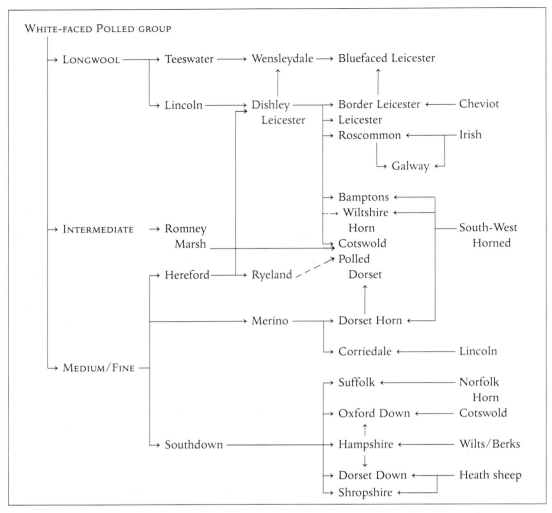

The second exotic group probably originated in Asia, and may owe at least part of its ancestry to the Argali wild sheep, but the date of its arrival in Britain is not known. It has remained much more distinct than other types and can most clearly be seen in such black-faced, horned hill breeds as the Swaledale and Scottish Blackface, with their long coarse fleece and spiralled horns.

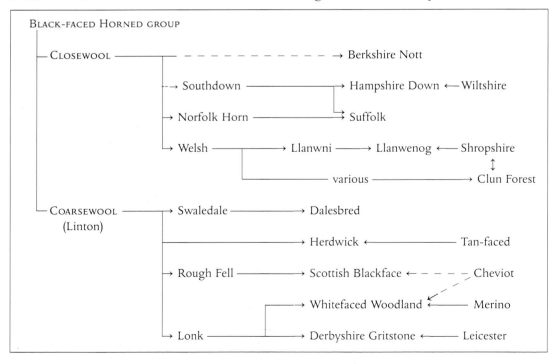

*'Changing Pastures'; a Victorian engraving after a painting by Rosa Bonheur of sheep being transported by boat off the west coast of Scotland*

As is the case with horses, the majority of sheep breeds originated from more than one basic type, and any attempt to unravel their ancestry inevitably leads to considerable oversimplification.

In the agriculture of Mesopotamia and Egypt one of the most important animals was the goat. It was derived from the wild bezoar or pasang goat *(Capra aegagrus)*, whose range extended from the Balkans through the Near East to the Indus valley. Although relatively pure specimens of the wild ancestral strain still remain in Crete, in general most of the extant non-domesticated animals are feral goats. This is especially true in the British Isles, where the herds of Old English goat have all arisen from domestic goats which escaped or were turned loose.

## Pigs

It is probable that the pig, too, was domesticated in the Near East, rather later than sheep, goats and cattle but earlier than the horse. There is some evidence to suggest a separate site of domestication in South-East Asia: the most important trade route of the ancient world, the Silk Road, stretched 6250 miles from the Chinese Pacific coast to the Mediterranean Sea, permitting a regular interchange of livestock and goods at all points along the way, and this could have mixed the two types at an early stage.

Attitudes in the ancient world to the pig were never moderate. Nomadic tribes despised it and made it the subject of religious prohibitions; even modern nomads, such as those of South America today, do not breed pigs. On the other hand, herds of pigs were valued in ancient Egypt for their ability to tread down reeds after flooding of the land and create a fertile seedbed for cultivated crops. In a similar manner, the animal's grubbing habits were turned to advantage by Greeks, Romans, Germans and Celts to transform woodland into rich farmland. 'Pigs were the bulldozers of antiquity, and sheep were the mowing machines which followed behind.'

The pigs found in Britain until the end of the eighteenth century were indigenous descendants of the European wild boar, *Sus scrofa*. During the Iron Age they were big, long-legged animals with

The Yorkshire Hog, which weighed 609·6 kg, was 300 cm long with a 244 cm girth, and stood 122·5 cm high at the withers. This type was the forerunner of the Large White breed. From an engraving by R. Pollard in 1809

large tusks, but later developed into a massive animal weighing over 450 kg. The large white breeds are derived directly from this pig, and the Tamworth can be included in the same category although its attractive reddish-gold colouring may result from the importation of the Red Barbadan pig from the West Indies. Late in the seventeenth century Chinese pigs were introduced, first into Italy and later into Britain. Some authorities believe that these pigs were descended from a separate wild species, *Sus vittatus,* and they have different blood groups. In contrast to the European pigs they were small, fat and prick-eared with a fine downy coat, and matured early. In Italy they became the black Neapolitan, which helped later in England to transform the large, rangy Berkshire with its

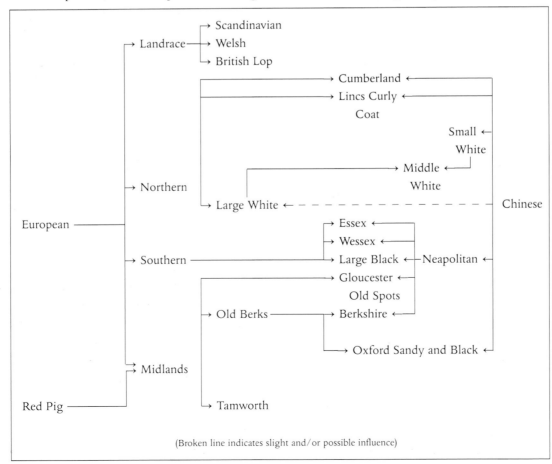

(Broken line indicates slight and/or possible influence)

sandy colouring and black markings into the modern compact black animal which bears the name today. The Chinese pigs directly imported to Britain are most nearly represented by the Middle White, which was derived from the more extreme, but now extinct, Small White. Most modern British breeds result from the mixture of native and Asian types. A second 'invasion' of Chinese pigs in the closing years of the twentieth century may be presaged by trials involving the Meishan variety of the Taihu pig. Despite its unprepossessing folds of fat-laden skin, its high fecundity and early maturity have encouraged breeders to exploit the hybrid vigour of its crosses with European breeds.

The origin of the belted pattern of the British Saddleback is not clear. The breed resulted from the recent amalgamation of the Essex and Wessex, but authoritative works written in the early

nineteenth century make no mention of belted pigs in England. There are authentic records of a belted pig, the Cinta Senese (*Siena Belted*) in Italy as early as AD 1339, when such an animal was depicted in a medieval painting, and I saw similar pigs during a visit to Tuscany in 1980.

*The Scots Grey was also known as the Cottagers Fowl. It is a hardy, alert and active breed that may have retained more of its utility characteristics than other native British breeds.*

## Poultry

It is probable that the Red Jungle Fowl is the ancestor of all modern breeds of chicken. Early selection in Asia seems to have been for both ornamental purposes and cock-fighting. The abundance of soft feather and the small wings of Asiatic breeds would indicate an ornamental function, but there are Chinese records of cock-fighting pre-1,000 BC. The birds from which the European breeds were descended probably were introduced to the Greeks by the Persians c.600 BC, while it is possible that a separate influence contributed to the development of Russian breeds.

There are five recognised types of wild turkey, but all domestic stock is descended from the Mexican (*Meleagris gallopavo gallopavo*). Birds of this type were taken to Spain by the Conquistadores in the early sixteenth century, and from there they spread through Europe to the British Isles, having been progressively domesticated in the process. They were returned to North America by the British from 1850 onwards during the period of colonisation.

Poultry were an integral part of most farmyards in Britain in earlier times, but they are now kept mainly as 'fancy fowl' or are selected within the programmes of the international breeding companies. The old, traditional, native breeds, which still exist in small numbers are the Scots Grey, Scots Dumpy, Old English Pheasant Fowl, Derbyshire Redcap, Dorking, Sussex and Cornish Game, plus a larger population of Old English Game.

## Other Species

Although the dog was among the earliest animals to be domesticated and may then have assisted in the capture and domestication of other species, the reindeer, which was used both for riding and as a draught animal, was probably the first. It inhabited Mongolia (with two other wild species of great importance to the human economy, the horse and the camel) and achieved wide distribution during the Ice Age, appearing abundantly in cave paintings at Lascaux and Altamira. Reindeer migrated northward as the ice receded and became confined in a small and specialised environment bordering the coniferous forests and tundra.

Britain thus possesses twenty-seven native breeds of cattle, fifty-three of sheep, two of goat, seventeen of horses and ponies, and nine of pig. They have been derived from widely contrasting foundation types and have evolved in varying conditions, each to suit a specific market demand. Their fortunes have fluctuated from century to century, and even decade to decade, but each breed possesses unique characteristics. They offer rich resources for animal breeders and geneticists in future generations.

# CHAPTER 3

# THE CONSERVATION
# OF MINORITY BREEDS

One of the arguments advanced with monotonous regularity by those who wish to rationalise the livestock industry is that the number of breeds should be reduced drastically. In theory, this suggestion has much to recommend it, if you consider the apparent extravagance of maintaining 108 native breeds of cattle, sheep, goats, pigs, horses and ponies in the relatively small compass of the British Isles, especially when foreign breeds can be imported with relative ease. But each breed fills a special niche, and its replacement by another might well result in a loss of efficiency. The most successful contemporary British breed of mountain sheep is the Swaledale, which is adapted to heather moorland. It is increasing its range at the expense of most other mountain breeds, yet even the Swaledale must yield to other breeds in such environments as the higher peaks of the Lake District, which are the domain of the Herdwick, or the old Silurian shales around Kendal and Sedbergh in Cumbria, to which the Rough Fell is especially adapted. Similarly, every other breed can point to particular areas or circumstances that justify its existence.

However, it is not sufficient to rely on the natural forces of commercial value or genetic merit to ensure a breed's survival. The equal powers of fashion and chance have introduced an illogical element into the fortunes of the individual breeds, creating the need for a deliberate policy of conservation for many. In recent decades the rate of change has increased, and conservation measures have become a more urgent need to prevent the forfeiture of unique and valuable genes. During the four years 1971–4 the number of British Saddleback litters notified to the National Pig Breeders' Association, (now the British Pig Association), dropped from 1278 in 1971 to 553 in 1974, and the figure for Large Black pigs fell from 194 to 56 – reductions of 57 per cent and 71 per cent respectively. Indeed, among pigs only the bacon type, represented by the Large White, and Landrace (the Welsh can be regarded as a variety of the Landrace) is numerically secure. The coloured and the hardy breeds, as well as the pork and dual-purpose breeds, are all endangered, as the registration and population figures show.

*Registrations of Minority Breeds of Pig*

| Breed | 1974 Boars | 1974 Gilts | 1986 Boars | 1986 Gilts |
|---|---|---|---|---|
| Middle White | 5 | 27 | 15 | 69 |
| Berkshire | 7 | 36 | 22 | 85 |
| British Lop | 14 | 58 | 24 | 84 |
| Tamworth | 11 | 32 | 24 | 102 |
| British Saddleback | 55 | 219 | 40 | 157 |
| Large Black | 18 | 55 | 50 | 158 |
| Gloucester Old Spots | 13 | 57 | 59 | 345 |

The situation is much the same among cattle. The Friesian/Holstein dominates the dairy and dual-purpose section to such an extent that all the other breeds are in some danger, while the Dairy Shorthorn, once the pride of British dairy farmers, seems destined to join the minority breeds before too long. Among beef breeds, all the native breeds have been eclipsed by the dramatic surge of exotic stock in the last ten years.

Those who attempt to justify genetic conservation on the grounds of sentiment are often regarded as eccentric, but why should the survival of our ancient breeds of domestic livestock be any less important than the preservation of historic buildings or rare plants? As a symbol of British national heritage Stonehenge is heavily guarded by public opinion. There is a case for giving equal recognition to the White Park cattle that were introduced almost 4000 years ago by the Beaker people, who may have been partly responsible, too, for the construction of Stonehenge. At a later date the history of the White Park cattle was again linked with that of Stonehenge in the sacrificial rituals of the Druids. The Cistercian monks, builders in the twelfth century of the great Yorkshire abbeys, were also accomplished farmers noted for their livestock: longwool sheep, white cattle, and

OPPOSITE:
*A group of Soay rams. Most parkland Soays were brought off the island of Soay before 1932, and their type has been fixed by selection on the mainland*

*A1 Demand in England and Wales (Milk Marketing Board Inseminations)*

| | | 1986–7 Number | 1986–7 % | 1976–7 % | 1966–7 % |
|---|---|---|---|---|---|
| **DAIRY AND DUAL-PURPOSE BREEDS** | | | | | |
| *Native* | Friesian/Holstein | 1071675 | 94.42 | 92.96 | 80.92 |
| | Jersey | 26355 | 2.32 | 2.28 | 5.20 |
| | Guernsey | 15599 | 1.37 | 2.38 | 6.71 |
| | Ayrshire | 14890 | 1.31 | 1.86 | 5.65 |
| | Dairy Shorthorn | 4496 | 0.40 | 0.44 | 1.36 |
| **EXOTIC** | | 1183 | 0.10 | 0.05 | 0.04 |
| *Minority* | Dexter | 361 | 0.03 | 0.01 | – |
| | Red Poll | 309 | 0.03 | 0.02 | 0.12 |
| | British White | 89 | 0.01 | – | – |
| | Gloucester | 42 | – | – | – |
| | Kerry | 14 | – | – | – |
| | Shetland | 11 | – | – | – |
| | | 1135024 | 100.00 | 100.00 | 100.00 |
| **BEEF BREEDS** | | | | | |
| *Native* | Hereford | 225584 | 20.58 | 61.13 | 61.75 |
| | Aberdeen Angus | 60579 | 5.53 | 11.92 | 19.30 |
| | Welsh Black | 6460 | 0.59 | 1.09 | 1.48 |
| | Sussex | 4451 | 0.41 | 0.82 | 0.73 |
| | Devon | 4213 | 0.38 | 1.70 | 3.66 |
| | South Devon | 3857 | 0.35 | 0.91 | 1.54 |
| | Lincoln Red | 562 | 0.05 | 0.15 | 0.11 |
| | Galloway | 56 | 0.01 | 0.14 | 0.28 |
| | Others | 190 | 0.02 | 0.11 | 0.05 |
| | | (305952) | (27.92) | (77.97) | (88.90) |
| *Exotic* | Limousin | 404419 | 36.90 | 1.52 | – |
| | Charolais | 204613 | 18.67 | 15.23 | 11.10 |
| | Belgian Blue | 78944 | 7.20 | – | – |
| | Simmental | 74208 | 6.77 | 3.23 | – |
| | Blonde d'Acquitaine | 18537 | 1.69 | – | – |
| | Murray Grey | 7684 | 0.70 | 1.41 | – |
| | Others | 1386 | 0.13 | 0.63 | – |
| | | (789791) | (72.06) | (22.02) | (11.10) |
| *Minority* | Longhorn | 115 | 0.01 | 0.01 | – |
| | Beef Shorthorn | 95 | 0.01 | 0.11 | 0.05 |
| | White Park | 50 | – | – | – |
| | | (260) | (0.02) | (0.12) | (0.05) |
| | | 1096003 | 100.00 | 100.00 | 100.00 |

Fell and Dales ponies probably represent more truly their contribution to British history than the preserved ruins of their famous abbeys.

Ideally, conservation programmes should incorporate a combination of valuable ingredients. This is achieved in a simple way when an endangered native breed is maintained in parkland surrounding an historic stately home. More recently there have been attempts in Britain to use rare breeds in agroecosystems, which are looked upon favourably within the European Community. On

ABOVE:
*Soay island in the St Kilda group. All present-day Soay sheep are descended from the flock on this island*

RIGHT:
*The late Mr Storey at Horning, Norfolk, with part of his flock of light-coloured Soays photographed pre-1961. Although Soay sheep do not react like other sheep to shepherding with dogs, they can become tame*

the mainland of Europe, Grey Steppe cattle on the Hungarian puszta and Camargue horses in the Rhone delta provided good examples. The dietary preferences of Hebridean sheep have been exploited on Skipwith Common near York, the Spurn Peninsular in Humberside, and Ainsdale in Lancashire, where they have proved superior to other breeds. Their browsing ability controlled and eradicated invasive birch scrub, creeping willow, Sea Buckthorn, and even the tough leathery Sea Purslane. This preference for coarser herbage has been noted in other breeds such as White Park cattle.

In some cases the co-operation of different interests is more difficult to obtain. When Exmoor was declared an Environmentally Sensitive Area the proposed management plan required all livestock to be removed from the moor during the winter months. This included the Exmoor Pony semi-feral herds that are the genetic base of the breed, and it shows that there remains a lack of understanding of the importance of the conservation of this aspect of our heritage.

Britain's ability to identify much of her history in extant breeds of livestock is the envy of many other nations. Soay sheep, which survived on the lonely islands of St Kilda, are a relic from the earliest stages of domestication. The name Soay means 'sheep island', and all Soay sheep on the island of Hirta are descended from 107 animals (20 rams, 44 ewes, 22 ram lambs and 21 ewe lambs) which were transferred by the Marquess of Bute from the almost inaccessible Soay island to Hirta in 1932, when the human population was evacuated. Previously a breeding group had been taken to Woburn c.1910.

One legacy of the religious wars which occupied English monarchs in the twelfth century was the introduction of Schwarzhal goats, which probably were brought back from the Rhone valley by a Crusader and allowed to run as a feral herd on the estate of the Staffordshire family from whom they take their British name, Bagot goats. The chargers ridden into battles of the same period were the old English War Horses, forerunners of today's Shire. Several herds of White Park cattle were enclosed in parks in the mid-thirteenth century, when the Plantagenet King Henry III accorded to certain barons the right to empark portions of the extensive forests as hunting chases, and remain now as a living link with the past.

Livestock continued to reflect British history in more recent times. The nation's agriculture was quick to adjust to the new dietary demands of an industrial society in the eighteenth century. John

LEFT:
*The Southdown was the native sheep of the South Downs in Sussex, and originally was fine-woolled, polled and blackfaced. It was improved by John Ellman of Glynde in the late eighteenth century, and later by Jonas Webb of Babraham near Cambridge*

BELOW LEFT:
*The long, lustrous, purly fleece and dark pigmented face are hallmarks of the Wensley-dale, seen here in its native area of Yorkshire. (Photo F Pedley)*

Ellman transformed the leggy native heath sheep of Sussex into the compact modern Southdown, while Robert Bakewell performed a similar task with Longhorn cattle and Leicester sheep. The Longhorn (not to be confused with the Hamitic Longhorn or the Texas Longhorn) became for a brief period the most popular breed of cattle in the British Isles, and both the Southdown and the Dishley Leicester exerted a profound influence on the development of sheep breeds throughout Europe. The changes achieved by these two breeders were accompanied by serious genetic losses, however: the Longhorn suffered diminished milking ability, and the Dishley Leicester and its descendants became less prolific.

Many of the breeds which are now rare have made a significant contribution to the development of popular and modern breeds, especially in the sheep industry. The Norfolk Horn was an ancestor

*A Westmorland shepherd carrying a Herdwick ewe, photographed by Joseph Hardman c.1920*

of the Suffolk, Britain's most popular meat sire; the Portland gave rise to the Dorset Horn with out-of-season breeding ability; the Lleyn was one of the breeds used in the formation of the British Milksheep, Britain's most prolific and milky breed; and the Lincoln, when crossed with the Merino, produced the Polwarth and the Corriedale in Australia. Similarly among pigs, the extinct Cumberland and Lincolnshire Curly Coat, together with the Yorkshire, were used to create the Chester White, which was imported from the USA by the British breeder Geoffrey Cloke, who was a major force in both the Rare Breeds Survival Trust and the British Pig Association.

In the future, it is likely that scientific or commercial considerations will replace sentiment as the main justification for the conservation of minority breeds. Many of these old breeds possess qualities which were not recognised in previous centuries. With today's detailed methods of evaluation and sophisticated scientific techniques, it is possible to analyse and define the characteristics of each breed more accurately. In studies of the effects on sheep of organophosphate compounds used in anthelmintics, it emerged that some breeds, including the Herdwick, can hydrolyse the compounds more rapidly than others, such as the Dorest Down, and are thus less subject to possible harmful effects. In contrast, negative qualities may be revealed: when attempts were made to save the Norfolk Horn with the use of ova-transfer techniques, the breed proved exceptionally resistant to hormone treatment and failed to super-ovulate. Similar failures were experienced in projects with Vaynol and Gloucester cattle. A good example of the part played by rare breeds in contemporary scientific research is the use of serum from Soay sheep in the detection of anabolic steroids used to enhance the performance of both racehorses and human athletes. Another fascinating subject is the unique physiological adaptation of the North Ronaldsay sheep to a diet of seaweed. It is impossible to discount the likelihood that many more valuable attributes will be discovered in breeds which are now out of fashion commercially.

The ability of some minority breeds to make a useful contribution to livestock production has already become clear, although it may take some time for their qualities to be appreciated more widely. The use of the Cleveland Bay as a carriage horse is well known, but the value of the White Park as the sire of beef calves, the maternal qualities of Large Black sows, and the efficiency of Hebridean ewes in crossbred lamb-production systems, deserve equal recognition. But it is the ever-changing pattern of livestock production that provides the strongest commercial reason for preserving a minority breed. For example, in the continuing fluctuation in the demand for lean meat or fat, lean meat is currently in favour and is increasing the popularity of previously unpopular breeds.

Most of the breeds which are popular today have been in a minority at some time in the past. The Wensleydale is one which has experienced the extremes of fortune, having first come to prominence as the sire of one of Britain's most popular and productive crossbred sheep, the Masham, and enjoyed considerable success. It was then superseded by the Teeswater, not for reasons of productivity but because its face colour was not considered fashionable. The Wensleydale's decline reached its lowest point in the late 1960s, when only 200 breeding ewes remained and it was on the verge of extinction. Nearly too late, the breed was suddenly recognised as the possessor of other valuable genes in addition to its prolificacy. Its strongly pigmented skin enables it to live in tropical climates, its large body size and the rapid growth rate of its progeny are well suited to the market for heavyweight lambs, and above all its wool is of a special quality. All these attributes enhance its future prospects and make it a fine example of the importance of conserving minority breeds for the benefit of future generations.

*A Lakeland shepherd bringing a flock down from the fells c.1900. Beatrix Potter bought Troutbeck Farm in 1923, and gave land in the Lake District to the National Trust on the condition that Herdwick sheep were kept there*

# CHAPTER 4

# ANIMALS AND MAN

# Livestock Improvement

Adetailed assessment of the history of animal breeding is a humbling experience, not because it suggests any lack of ability on the part of the great livestock breeders in the past, but rather because it reveals the human tendency to neglect lasting benefits in the achievement of short-term gains. In his intensive breeding programmes, Man can manipulate genetic material with alarming speed. The diversity of modern dog breeds is evidence enough of the effectiveness of selective breeding. All of them, from the massive Mastiff to the miniature Chihuahua, from the broad-chested Bulldog to the lean and hungry Greyhound, have been derived from a common ancestor. Their evolution took several thousand years, but the speed of change in animal breeding has increased dramatically over the last two centuries. In 1793 when the Colling brothers, two progressive farmers from Teesside, visited Robert Bakewell at Dishley Grange, the cattle of Durham and North Yorkshire belonged to a single type known as the Durham or Teeswater. Within 150 years this type was developed by the Collings' successors into several distinct breeds, with the squat Beef Shorthorn at one extreme and the hardy, light-framed Northern Dairy Shorthorn at the other.

There should be no aversion to change, and rapid change can be highly desirable provided that it leads to improvement, but it would be dangerous to assume that change and improvement are synonymous. Ever since animals were first domesticated 10,000 or more years ago, Man has sought to impose his concepts and ideals on the evolution of domestic livestock. Before then the adaptation of animals to their natural environment was determined by the survival of the fittest; afterwards, Man's selection of his domestic livestock emphasised characteristics which increasingly removed animals from their original habitat. Artificial systems became the environment in which livestock evolved, and breeding programmes have helped to hasten the process.

The artificial environments created by Man have reached extreme development in the case of many modern pig and poultry enterprises, where scientifically formulated diets are delivered automatically at regular intervals in housing which exerts full artificial control of temperature and humidity, but provides the smallest permissible amount of space. Under such circumstances animals lose the ability to fend for themselves: neither their instincts nor their physique would enable them to cope with the conditions in which their ancestors lived. Feeding and housing are only the first stage – their effect is compounded by the widespread and often indiscriminate use of drugs and vaccines to control disease, and of hormones to increase litter size and boost milk yield.

The Landrace pigs of Scandinavia have been considered the acme of selective pig breeding. Their conformation is a geneticist's dream: with bodies as long as the formulae that were used to computerise their breeding, they slot neatly into the standard pattern of pig production which has been too readily accepted as the ideal in western Europe. Superficially the notion seems plausible, and a newcomer to the pig industry might be forgiven for accepting without too much question the great quantity of propaganda that urges him to conform. It may be that human pride is part of the problem: the Landrace pig is the realisation of an ideal, and the conviction of its rightness is deeply ingrained in breeders and scientists alike. They have reacted very slowly to the warning signs that maybe the body has become so long that in some pigs the hind legs no longer function efficiently, or that the extreme emphasis on the animal's shape has led to deterioration in meat quality.

The meat of popular breeds such as the Hampshire, Duroc, Large White, Landrace and Pietrain, is inferior to that of the rare breeds for colour of the meat, setting of the joint, grain of the muscle and, of particular importance, loss of exudate. The last quality is closely associated with Pig Stress Syndrome (PSS): economically this characteristic is linked with a higher killing-out percentage and a greater proportion of lean meat in the carcass, but these advantages are far outweighed by the loss of meat quality, especially PSE (pale, soft and exudative), and stress deaths. The incidence of PSS is very high (up to 100%) in the Pietrain and some strains of Landrace, but is absent in the rare breeds. As PSS seems to be a single-gene effect, it may be possible to manipulate its frequency by progeny testing or even to eliminate it by genetic engineering, but in view of the increasing

OPPOSITE:
*Having been replaced by imported breeds to an alarming and unjustified extent, the Nguni is now re-asserting itself in South Africa. Its superior efficiency of production is determined by its native adaptability, tick-resistance and ease of calving*

ABOVE LEFT:
*Landrace pig. A breed developed for intensive systems of bacon production, and selected for a minimum thickness of backfat*

ABOVE:
*Broad-breasted White Turkey. This breed has been so overdeveloped for meat production that it is unable to mate naturally because of its shape, and relies entirely on artificial insemination*

concern with meat quality the use of genes from traditional rare breeds in commercial hybrids may be a more sensible way of restoring a better sense of perspective to the pig industry.

Pale watery meat and other undesirable consequences of popular breeding methods in themselves pose a serious problem, but even more serious are the financial implications for those breeds that rely on expensive housing and high-energy diets. It may be that the pig industry has reached a dead end and needs to return to a point from which it can re-appraise breeds that thrive in outdoor systems, foraging for themselves and reducing to a minimum direct competition with humans for food.

The name Landrace means 'native breed', and it might be expected that the breeds from Scandinavia would be hardy, thrifty and fully adapted to difficult climatic conditions. In practice this is not always so, because Scandinavian winters are so severe that animals are housed. Thus because they were controlled closely and housed during pregnancy, Finnish Landrace sheep were developed as a prolific breed, but at the same time their wool lost its ability to shed water, so that they cannot tolerate a wet climate, and they have a carcass of low quality, feet which are susceptible to disease, and a poor jaw and tooth structure. Other imported breeds of sheep, such as the Bleu du Maine and the Friesland, have proved equally delicate in various ways. Most of these deficiencies must be marked down among the debits in a critical account of artificial selection. It is difficult to justify the financial extravagance which has surrounded the importation by British breeders of foreign breeds, when native breeds often are genetically superior. For example, imported breeds of sheep cannot compare with the ability of the Oxford Down to sire heavyweight lamb of good conformation, nor with the British Milksheep's combination of prolificacy, milk yield and a large lean carcass.

In some cases the disadvantages are more drastic. Charolais and Belgian Blue cattle have both enjoyed increased popularity because of their growth rate and conformation, but these are associated with a condition of hypertrophied muscles, known as culard or doublemuscling, which causes difficult calvings. Rapid growth rate is of no value unless a live calf is reared; in the speculative fervour that magnifies the reputation of imported breeds, insufficient attention is paid to their defects. Charolais cattle cause difficult calvings with associated damage to the cows and produce coarse-grained meat; the Limousin has a volatile temperament and is difficult to finish off grass; the Belgian Blue is bedevilled by Caesarian births and its flesh is very tough.

*A British Milksheep ewe, Gallowshieldrigg Melody 70th, with her quadruplet lambs; she reared 13 lambs in 4 crops and had a milk yield rating of 20.9% above the breed average of 400 litres per lactation*

It is significant that all the breeds here illustrating the undesirable effects of artificial selection were developed for one particular major production characteristic. The value of these features has resulted in the breeds' export to many parts of the world, often to areas for which they were unsuitable, and always taking with them the unwanted side-effects. A solution might be found in selection within these breeds to eradicate the undesirable characteristics, but usually they are so closely linked to other factors that such a programme would not be feasible. An alternative approach is to take the natural environment as the starting point, selecting breeds that are suited to it. It might be called the ecological approach, with emphasis on efficiency rather than maximum production. Such a system contrasts sharply with the current search for animals or breeds with the highest yield, and adapting the environment, usually at great cost, to suit them. Exotic breeds, riding on the crest of a short-lived wave of speculation, are less likely to thrive than indigenous breeds. It was fashionable in British agriculture of the eighteenth century to use the imported fine-

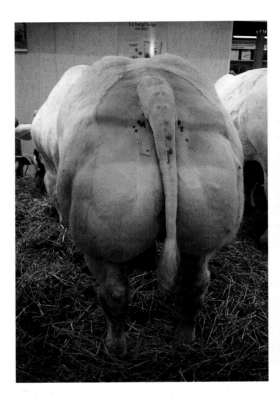

woolled Merino, but the breed failed miserably to tolerate British conditions and its long-term effect on the British sheep industry was negligible.

Within the ecological approach there are two possible courses of action. We may escape from the present impasse by returning to breeds which have not been diverted from the path of natural development. Those that are widely described as unimproved and primitive have retained many of the qualities which were bred out of more popular breeds. Alternatively, we can return to the very beginning of domestication and attempt to utilise other species of wild animals in the hope that earlier mistakes can be avoided.

ABOVE LEFT:

*The hindquarters of a Belgian Blue showing the extreme hypertrophied muscles found in this breed of cattle, and also in the Piedmontese and Charolais and some other breeds to a lesser degree*

ABOVE:

*Charolais bullocks in their native pastures in France in 1966*

## Wild Genes

Since earliest times livestock breeders have tapped the vitality of wild animals by enabling wild males to cover their female breeding stock. It was particularly common among nomadic people, such as the Turkoman horse-herders, who came by their finest foals by turning out mares at night to be covered by wild stallions, full of quality, that came down from the mountains. Eskimoes allow their dogs to breed with wolves in order to maintain their strength and courage, while domestic poultry have regularly been crossed with wild jungle fowl in South-East Asia. Wild boars are still introduced to domestic stock in Asia, a practice which occurred until relatively recent times also in Europe. The introduction of wild genes into tame populations has thus been a feature of animal breeding throughout the whole process of domestication, implicitly admitting the deficiencies of artificial selection. It would be foolish to deny that progress has been achieved in the improvement of our domestic livestock, but equally it would be short-sighted not to recognise the defects and to explore all possible ways of remedying them. The use of wild genes is one possibility.

For several decades plant breeders have successfully increased the range of genetic material at their disposal by introducing wild strains. They have done this either by grafting wild stock on domestic varieties, or by domesticating new species. At the Welsh Plant Breeding Station at Aberystwyth the oat variety, Manod, acquired resistance to mildew by grafting on it genes from wild *Avena barbata* plants found in Algeria and at Rome airport. The alternative approach has been adopted by the Commonwealth Potato Collection at Edinburgh. Cultivated potatoes were developed from the very limited selection of maybe only a dozen wild types brought back from America by the early explorers. This narrow genetic base has accounted for the slow progress of potato breeding, with varieties such as King Edward, bred in 1902, and Majestic, bred in 1911, maintaining a dominant position for more than half a century. The Commonwealth Potato Collection now has amassed a unique genetic bank of 1200 potato species gathered from Central and South America, and is domesticating new species. In the United Kingdom the government has provided financial support for Kew Gardens, the vegetable gene bank at Wellesbourne and the National Fruit Collection at Brogdale. In Decorah, Iowa, Kent Whealy has developed a network ('Save our Seeds') to trace and conserve old varieties brought to the New World by early emigrants from Europe.

However, there are fundamental differences between plant and animal breeding that make the application of these techniques much more difficult in livestock improvement. The complicated chromosomal structure of animals and their long generation interval present serious problems. Theoretically it would seem that the injection of wild genes into our domestic stock would be a more feasible suggestion that the domestication of entirely new species. R. V. Short has argued that Embden or Toulouse geese might be improved by crossing with the wild Greater Snow Goose or the Red-breasted Goose, which have a shorter incubation period of only 23–24 days, a high efficiency of food conversion, and a very rapid growth rate. Similarly, crossing domestic sheep with the wild Argali, which stands up to 118 cm at the shoulder – higher than a Dexter bull – and weighs up to 200 kg, might be expected to result in better feed conversion, higher growth rate and increased hardiness. Evidence to support these claims is sparse, however, and the only major attempt to hybridise wild and domestic species for commercial purposes is found in the use of the American bison to create new 'breeds' of cattle.

The American bison, widely but incorrectly called the Buffalo, is beautifully adapted to the prairie lands of North America where it must overcome the effects of wind, snow and blizzards in winter, and the high summer temperatures of a continental climate. The bison has a fine inner coat which retains body heat, and a dense outer protective coat which protects all the vital organs. The testes, carried in a very small scrotum, are drawn into the body cavity during the severe winter cold. Only with the arrival of warmer spring weather do they drop into the scrotum, thus rendering the animal fertile.

Bison-cattle hybrids, known variously as 'Cattalo', 'Beefalo' and the 'American Breed', are claimed to have several advantages. They have better survival ability in exposed conditions, better resistance to disease, fewer calving difficulties, more efficient feed conversion, and a higher proportion of lean meat in the carcass. These are powerful commendations, but they are cancelled out by one overriding disadvantage: Mr Art Jones, the New Mexico rancher who developed the 'American Breed', admitted that half-bison bulls are always sterile, that infertility prevails in quarter- and three-quarterbreds, and that fertility in most bulls can only be expected when there is less than 25 per cent bison ancestry. The explanation probably has nothing to do with chromosomal incompatibility; it is more likely that the small scrotum of bison bulls is inherited by their part-bred progeny and holds the testes close to the body, at too high a temperature for fertility.

Despite the tantalising inducements to introduce wild genes into cattle from the bison the value of part-bison cattle to the livestock industry does not look promising, and I. L. Mason (1975) concluded that the available information did not substantiate claims for the superiority of these animals over domestic cattle. A more fruitful search for new genes might be made among feral stock. The herd of cattle in Chillingham Park, not far from the Scottish border, has roamed wild within its present enclosure since 1270. It is thought that no outside blood has been introduced, and the cattle have reverted to wild behaviour patterns, killing any calves that have been handled by humans. The herd forms a unique 'gene bank' that has evolved in a largely natural environment. Artificial selection has been applied only through the castration of bull calves and the culling of cows in the nineteenth century, by winter feeding since the park was reduced in size during the Second World War, by the provision of extra magnesium following the deaths of twenty-four animals from hypomagnesaemia in 1980, and by one park keeper who in 1770 deliberately eliminated

### The *WILD BULL*,

### OF THE ANCIENT CALEDONIAN BREED, NOW IN THE PARK AT CHILLINGHAM-CASTLE, NORTHUMBERLAND. 1789.

all the animals with black points, so that today the cattle are uniformly red-pointed and lyre-horned. They provide a potentially accessible source of genes that have bypassed the selection procedures of more than thirty generations of cattle breeders. The future of these cattle has been insured by the Sir James Knott Charitable Trust, which in 1981 granted the herd a 999-year lease on the park. A reserve herd has been established near Banff in Scotland. The search could be extended to other feral stocks, many of which are found on islands such as Ossabaw pigs (USA), Hog Island sheep (USA), Santa Cruz Island sheep (USA), Arapawa Island sheep (NZ) and Sable Island ponies (Canada).

It seems unlikely that the domestication of new species in the temperate climates of Europe or North America would meet with the same success as that of the Eland (*Taurotragus oryx*) or Grant's gazelle (*Gazella granti*) in East Africa. Cattle particularly, and sheep to a lesser degree, the most important domestic species in the temperate areas, are well adapted to their habitat. In addition,

*Chillingham bull. A wood engraving by Thomas Bewick, 1789*

farming wild species such as bison or wild boar must operate within strict and expensive safety regulations designed for zoo animals. Nevertheless, projects have been initiated to assess the feasibility of farming red deer (Blaxter *et al.* 1974). The great advantage claimed for red deer over most domesticated livestock is their ability to produce red meat; lamb carcasses contain three times as much fat as deer carcasses. However, they are equally efficient in the production of lean meat, as the energy used by lambs to produce fat is no greater than the energy lost as heat by deer. There is also some doubt over the ease with which they can be domesticated: deer have no submissive behaviour pattern, which is an important ingredient of domestication, and their territorial habits and lack of social structure make their management more difficult. Early experience indicated that calves born in captivity but reared on their dams are less tame than their dams, themselves bottle-reared.

Compared with sheep, red deer have a lower reproductive rate, and their maintenance feed requirement is about 30 per cent higher than that of sheep of the same weight. Nor are red deer immune from the ailments that plague domestic stock: they suffer from the full range of endoparasites – stomach and intestinal worms, lungworms, liver fluke and tapeworms. In 1881 half the herd at Welbeck Abbey was lost from lungworm, while a surprising number of wild Scottish stags are heavily infested with liver fluke. Ectoparasites, such as warble fly, head fly and nasal bot fly, also afflict deer, in addition to problems as serious as tuberculosis or Johne's disease, or as time-consuming as the need to trim their feet. Clearly the salvation of the world's food problems by the domestication of new species of livestock is not straightforward.

## Unimproved Breeds

Rather than start the whole process of domestication again with new species, a more acceptable solution might be to utilise the feral and domestic stocks which have suffered least from artificial selection, and may be expected to have retained many of the qualities that are desirable in wild animals. Virtually all breeds of domestic livestock have been subjected at some stage to a significant degree of artificial selection. Perhaps the most notable exception is the Soay sheep, the primitive breed that survives on the now-uninhabited St Kilda group of islands lying on the extreme periphery of the British Isles. Small groups of the sheep have been brought to the mainland at various times, to augment the aesthetic attractions of country parks, and in this way the Soay came to be regarded as an agricultural irrelevance. It is only since 1970 that a serious, objective evaluation of the breed has been made. The results are a devastating comment on 10,000 years of domestication and livestock improvement.

Since Bakewell and Ellman demonstrated their ability as livestock breeders to cater for the fat-loving palates developed by manual labourers with high-energy demands during the Industrial Revolution, dietary preferences in industrialised countries have come to favour lean meat. It is not surprising that the Soay, bypassed by the popular fashions of the last 200 years, is better able to meet this demand than the more popular breeds. According to a pattern of tissue growth to which sheep breeds conform closely, an animal lays down excess fat when it reaches about 50 per cent of its mature weight. Sheep differing as widely as the lean, bony Finnish Landrace and the compact, fat Down breeds fit the pattern – but not the Soay, which continues to lay down lean meat to greater weights.

The Soay is a small animal, with adult ewes weighing only about 25 kg. Body size substantially determines requirements of feed, the major input cost in any livestock enterprise, and the Soay shows up favourably in breed comparisons based on efficiency of production, i.e. output in relation to input. Labour is another major cost in orthodox sheep enterprises, and here again an 'easy management' breed such as the Soay scores heavily. Natural selection has ensured that there are few problems at lambing time and an almost complete absence of footrot, while the natural shedding of the wool obviates shearing costs. We might expect the breed to play a valuable role in remote areas of low fertility, where its ability to utilise poor quality herbage and to withstand predators in the absence of conventional shepherding can be used to greatest effect. The Soay has been used successfully in the reclamation of gravel pits in the Thames valley and china clay waste-tips in Cornwall – working examples of the unique genes of an unimproved domestic breed turned to good account in contemporary production systems.

The Tamworth pig cannot claim to have remained as free from 'improving' influences as the Soay, but it has retained more than other breeds of pig the valuable qualities of its wild ancestor. It is commonly believed that the pig is naturally a forest animal, using undergrowth for shelter and concealment, and no doubt this idea was fostered in Saxon and medieval times by the exercise of the rights of pannage. This characteristic is still exploited in Spain by the Iberian pigs in the oak forests of Extremadura. In fact, the wild pig was adapted to habitats as varied as forest and semidesert, steppes or marsh, provided that its requirements of water and cover were met. The Tamworth appears to have inherited this vital quality of adaptability: on the one hand it has been able to tolerate the hot, humid conditions of South-East Asia and the islands of the East Indies and Pacific Ocean; on the other, a herd of Tamworth pigs thrived outdoors very successfully in northern Scotland.

As with Soay sheep, renewed interest in the self-reliant Tamworth and other hardy pig breeds partly results from the high cost of foodstuffs and labour, but in the case of pigs there is the added incentive in the almost prohibitive cost of controlled environment housing, for which the popular breeds have been developed. Furthermore, it would be prudent to devise methods of pig production which minimise the potential competition between humans and pigs for food, and a more efficient system can hardly be imagined than one which operated in southern England where Tamworth sows ran in hillside scrubland with no housing, and obtained half their food requirement by grubbing and foraging. A level of production comparable with that of intensively managed animals was achieved with them. The Tamworth's attractive golden-brown colour gives protection against the sun, whereas the white breeds comprising more than 90 per cent of the pig population in the British Isles are susceptible to sunburn, and are also less suitable for field systems as they have so little fat that they lose condition outdoors. Another quality that the Tamworth shares with the Soay is that of high meat quality. Before the Second World War it enjoyed a good reputation in the Midlands of England as a producer of quality pork, while in North America it was used in breeding programmes to introduce carcass quality into a new breed, the Minnesota No. 1 (Winters).

The closest counterparts of the Soay among cattle are domesticated members of the White Park breed and the Texas Longhorn, which possess qualities of longevity, disease resistance, strong maternal instincts and a lean carcass. But there are several other breeds which fall to a lesser degree into the same category. The Kerry, Galloway and Shetland are all hardy, thrifty breeds which have evolved under unfavourable conditions.

The Shetland is unusual in several respects. On its native islands it is a small animal – a detailed account written in 1912 gives the weight of an adult cow as 290 kg. Moved to a less exposed site in northern Scotland, but still kept on poor-quality moorland, the animals increased in weight to about 450 kg, while in southern England Shetland cows may weigh up to 530 kg at maturity, although the average weight is 470 kg. It is difficult to assess their potential mature weight on good pasture properly because they convert their feed so efficiently that they quickly become too fat. Under the more amenable mainland environment there is a danger that the breed will be selected for greater size, and this is evident already in bulls such as Araclett Heracles and Tanyard Taurus, which are too large. In co-operation with the Breed Society, the Rare Breeds Survival Trust is now measuring the withers height of bulls before collecting semen, and encouraging the use of bulls of correct island type such as Trondra Thorgeir, Stanemore Odin and Waterloo Charlie. Cows should have a maximum withers height of 128 cm.

The ability of the breed to achieve a good milk yield and fatten easily under difficult conditions has been noted since Shetland cattle came to the attention of the earliest agricultural commentators. The calves receive no special treatment, and a group weaned on rough moorland and fattened on moderate pasture in Scotland were slaughtered at an average of 860 days of age with an average

TOP LEFT:
*A Texas Longhorn steer*

ABOVE:
*Soay sheep on waste tips at the English China Clay mines at St Austell in Cornwall, showing their use in reclamation projects*

TOP RIGHT:
*A Tamworth sow with litter. The breed is hardy but not very fecund*

BELOW RIGHT:
*Shetland cattle on their native Islands during the drought of 1976*

carcass weight of 295 kg – not an outstanding daily gain in carcass weight, but achieved under conditions which many high-performance breeds would not survive. Milk production records for the breed are limited, but a heifer calf, Foula of Ash, achieved a 200–day weight of 200 kg, which is higher than the average for female calves of any other British hill breed, although her mother was then only a heifer providing extra milk as a house cow. In its native islands, the Shetland is known as a 'clouty cow'. This name arose because the cows became so attached to their handler, usually the crofter's wife who was responsible for hand-milking the cattle, that it was necessary for a cow to be accompanied on sale by a square from her previous owner's apron (i.e. a clout), otherwise she would not accept her new situation. My own Shetland heifer, Rosemary 3rd, did not prove amenable to hand-milking, and she did not bring a clout with her!

The characteristic shared by Soay sheep, Tamworth pigs and Shetland cattle is their efficiency of production, based on their ability to thrive on relatively small amounts of lower-quality feed. Despite the apparent glut of food in the surpluses within the EEC which have prompted a policy of subsidies for non-production, the area of productive agricultural land is shrinking both in Britain and in the rest of the world. In the United Kingdom agricultural land has been lost to urban development and forestry at an annual rate of 69,000 hectares (Centre for Agricultural Strategy 1976). In other countries, the desert is encroaching alarmingly on fertile land. Degradation of land, mainly as a result of overgrazing, deforestation and unsustainable farming systems, is severely affecting 1.2 billion acres of the world. In the last fifty years, a part of the world equal in area to half the South American continent has become desert, and the famines in Africa as well as food shortages in the former Soviet Union, are a dramatic reminder of the vulnerability of the global food-supply position. Although 'desert creep' is mainly a problem of Africa and Asia, its effect throughout the world will be to accentuate the need for more efficient use of the remaining agricultural land.

Thus several factors – the national and international wastage of productive agricultural land, the need not to allow livestock to compete with humans for available feed supplies, the need not to rely too heavily on limited resources of energy such as artificial fertilisers, combine to place an important responsibility for livestock production on those breeds which can more efficiently utilise the remaining resources. In this context the Soay, the Tamworth and the Shetland deserve at least the same measure of attention as Finnish Landrace sheep, Landrace pigs and Charolais cattle.

## Special Environments

There are other minority breeds which have become adapted to unusual conditions. The island of North Ronaldsay is the northernmost of the Orkney group. Its cultivated land is separated from the foreshore by a high stone wall. There is no grass outside the wall, except for a small close-cropped area at the northernmost end of the island near the lighthouse. Nevertheless, the North Ronaldsay sheep spend most of the year on the shore, providing one of the most dramatic examples of adaptation to a highly specialised environment. The sheep are in groups, each of which stays voluntarily on its own area of the beach, known as a clowgang, and they are gathered ('punded') three times a year into nine punds which have been built at intervals along the wall. In February they are gathered for counting, and the owners are able to identify their animals by the ear notches. Between June and August the sheep are shorn, producing on average 1.1 kg of wool, though the yield of clean wool may be reduced to half this amount by contamination of the fleece by sand. The third gathering takes place at New Year, when animals are culled for killing. They are small, and even the carcass of a mature wether is unlikely to weigh more than 13.5 kg. The North Ronaldsay is unusual among British sheep in being better fed in winter than in summer, for the richest harvest of seaweed is thrown up on the beaches by the violent winter storms. Several breeds of sheep, cattle and pony, as well as deer, are able to utilise seaweed as part of their diet, but only the North Ronaldsay can thrive on it exclusively. The main part of their diet is kelp *(Laminaria digitata)*, although preferred species are *Rhodymenia palmata, Alaria esculentia* and *Palmaria palmata.* All these are found at low tide, but the sheep ignore the wrack species near the high-tide line. It appears that their preferences coincide closely with the nutritional values of the different species of seaweed.

The physiology of these sheep has undergone significant changes in the process of adaptation to their peculiar diet. Compared with Clun Forest sheep, the North Ronaldsay digests seaweed 12–15 per cent more efficiently, but the Clun Forest digests grass 55 per cent more efficiently. Blood and milk samples taken from a group of North Ronaldsay ewes thirty days after they were removed from their native island were analysed by standard metabolic profile techniques and compared with the values suggested by Payne (1970). The most significant feature was the high level of blood urea, with all samples falling outside the confidence levels for good health, although the total protein values were normal and the animals appeared in good health. Iodine levels in the milk of the North Ronaldsay ewes were 550 times those accepted as normal in mainland sheep (Hindson 1976), and the animals had to be restricted to a grass diet for more than two years before the iodine content fell to normal levels. It has been suggested that the high level of iodine in the body may help to control diseases such as mastitis or footrot. Another more fundamental change arises from the presence in seaweed of a factor which inhibits the body's absorption of dietary copper. North

Ronaldsay sheep have of necessity developed the ability to utilise copper four times more efficiently than other breeds of sheep, and some groups have suffered a high rate of mortality as a result of copper toxicity when taken off a seaweed diet.

The North Ronaldsay is closely related to the Finnish Landrace; both belong to the Northern short-tailed group of breeds. The shared relationship is expressed in a slender, fine-boned conformation, but the breeds have diverged markedly in their hardiness. While the Finnish Landrace has grown soft in the luxury of winter housing, the North Ronaldsay has had to endure the direct blast of rain-laden gales from the Atlantic, the North Sea and the Arctic region. It has developed a remarkable capacity to thrive under such conditions, even to the extent of wading into the sea twice a day in search of kelp – an ability comparable to that of the Northern Great Horse (second of the ancestral types as defined by Ebhardt) which could stand in swamps to feed on plants submerged in icy water.

The wool of the North Ronaldsay sheep contributes significantly to the breed's hardiness. Although basically fine, it forms next to the skin a dense mat which is not removed when the sheep are shorn. It had been assumed that the North Ronaldsay would shed its wool naturally, but a group of 114 ewes and seven rams transferred to the 57.5-hectare island of Linga Holm in August 1974 were not shorn until July 1976, by which time scarcely any animal had cast its fleece.

The Orkney and Shetland Islands suffer a similar degree of exposure to harsh weather, and most of their native breeds of livestock are stunted. Judging by the rapid increase in the size of Shetland cattle when moved to kinder pastures, we might deduce that conditions on the islands were responsible for the small size of the animals. However, the evidence so far available on the transfer of North Ronaldsay sheep does not support this theory. The sheep moved to Riber Castle in Derbyshire in the 1960s have not increased in size, and their progeny, born and reared in the relative luxury of the English countryside, have tended to be smaller than the foundation stock. This evidence must be interpreted with care, as nutritional factors may be involved. Historically Derbyshire was notorious for the high incidence in its human population of goitre resulting from iodine deficiency, and the local mineral imbalance may have had an adverse effect on a breed accustomed to an abnormally high level of iodine. However, information from other mainland flocks and from Linga Holm, where the sheep have adequate access to both kelp and grass as well as much more effective shelter than that available on their native island, indicates that the mature body weight of the sheep is not increasing, although the lamb growth-rates may be higher.

The flock on Linga Holm was established as an easy management unit kept to some degree on a random breeding basis to conserve genetic variability. A working party, under the leadership of Ken and Nancy Briggs, visits the island in the summer each year to apply the parasite control programme, shear the flock, and take off those animals which are to be culled. Animals with defects are culled, and the flock is maintained at about 25 rams and 175 ewes and their followers, including a full range of colour types. Gathering is a difficult operation as the North Ronaldsay does not follow all the normal patterns of sheep behaviour. The original warden appointed by the Rare Breeds Survival Trust, Sam Cooper, reporting on the efforts of eleven men to round up the flock for shearing in 1976, described it as 'pandemonium', and the following year 105 sheep out of a total of 828 escaped during the gather.

The temperament of the sheep may be a disadvantage in some ways, but it is an important factor in ensuring the breed's survival. Before the introduction of the North Ronaldsay flock, Linga Holm was stocked with Cheviot sheep, which were shepherded in a more conventional manner, but they suffered from the plunder of each crop of new-born lambs by Greater Black-backed gulls without any strong protest from the ewes, so that only about forty lambs were reared. The gulls faced a different reception when the aggressive North Ronaldsay ewes arrived; very few lambs were lost, and a good proportion of the ewes reared twins, so that now more than 250 lambs are reared on the island each year. Lambing starts on about 28 April and occurs mainly in May, so that the lambs avoid the worst conditions of late winter and early spring but are only five months old when the first serious violence of the winter storms breaks out.

*North Ronaldsay sheep on their native island in the Orkney archipelago wading into the sea to obtain the seaweed which is their exclusive diet for most of the year*

In the North Ronaldsay sheep, therefore, we have a hardy, specialist breed adapted to an extremely unusual environment. It is difficult to visualise a wider role for them within the sheep industry, although the ability to utilise seaweed may assume greater significance as more grassland disappears under housing estates, motorways, industrial expansion and, on the hill sheep walks, forests as the Forestry Commission encroaches increasingly on the beautiful upland and mountain areas. Interest has been expressed in the meat of the North Ronaldsay. The tang of the sea gives it a special appeal, and specialist outlets are being developed that may give the breed the impetus it requires to establish itself on a more secure footing.

Several thousand miles away, another breed has started to take the first critical steps back into the main thoroughfare of the American cattle industry. During the 500 years since the first Spanish cattle landed in the Americas, their descendants have become identified with the romantic history of North America as closely as the Toro de Lidia or fighting bull is associated with Spain. Their moment of glory coincided with that glamorous period in American history of pioneers, cowboys and cattle trails, and they are etched in our memory as the Texas Longhorns.

After the bison had been hunted from its historic grazing grounds, the prairies were among many areas repopulated mainly by the Texas Longhorn. Originally these cattle were variable in appearance, particularly with regard to colour, but they had become sufficiently distinct by the middle of the nineteenth century to be called a breed, 'though not one of all their progenitors ever had his name enrolled in a herd book or his ear tagged with a brass number'. The value of the breed results from this absence of a registration during its formative stage, which allowed it to adapt naturally to all the areas it populated. Wherever the early Spanish explorers went they took horses and cattle with them, and in colonial times it was their custom to leave most of the males entire, so that the feral 'mustang' stock descended from these animals possessed a broad genetic base and 'were all the colours of the rainbow'. Natural selection pays no regard to a visually pleasing conformation and, as Dobie recorded,

> for all his heroic stature, the Texas steer stood with his body tucked up in the flanks, his high shoulder-top sometimes thin enough to split a hailstone, his ribs flat, his length frequently so extended that his back swayed. Viewed from the side, his big frame would fool a novice into a ridiculous over-estimate of his weight, but a rear view was likely to show cat hams, narrow hips, and a ridgepole kind of backbone.... But however they appeared, with their steel hooves, their long legs, their staglike muscles, their thick skins, their powerful horns, they could walk the roughest ground, cross the widest

deserts, climb the highest mountains, swim the widest rivers, fight off the fiercest bands of wolves, endure hunger, cold, thirst and punishment as few beasts of the earth have ever shown themselves capable of enduring.

What a vivid picture this paints of a self-reliant, independent breed on a grand scale! The North Ronaldsay ewes resist the predations of gulls, but Texas Longhorn cows could cope with a pack of marauding wolves. However, as the open plains were fenced in and it became fashionable to introduce Durham and, later, Hereford cattle, the Texas Longhorn lost favour and exotic European stock replaced the native breed. Despite the danger of extinction, the Longhorn obstinately survived and, after a century of discrimination against it, the breed's unique qualities are once again becoming available to the American cattle industry.

The strong maternal instincts aroused in Texas Longhorn cows by wolves and other predators in the past are no less valuable today. The cows give birth with little trouble, and the calves are quickly on their feet and active. Under tough range conditions, their high fertility again reflects the value of their natural evolution, in which the fittest were characterised by hardiness, adaptability, and resistance to disease and parasites. These cattle are noted for their longevity, with cows not infrequently breeding up to 25 years of age. But most important of all, they are the 'thriftiest rustlers' of any breed, with their ability to utilise the high browse and coarse forage of the marginal rangelands; their mouths are hard enough to feed on the cactus that enables them to survive in drought conditions. With changing economic circumstances it is possible that the Texas Longhorn, rough-hewn by the ruthless forces of the West, can resume the role that it played one hundred years ago, provided that the purity of its breeding is respected and maintained with increasing popularity.

In view of the effects of adverse environments in the development of North Ronaldsay sheep and Texas Longhorn cattle, fertile lowlands and lush grazing might be expected to provide a suitable medium for the development of large breeds with a high level of production. There is a region where such conditions, combined with the skill of the inhabitants as animal breeders, have produced not one but three large, high-performance breeds. Out of the rich alluvial basin approximating to the Low Countries have come the massive black Flemish horse that formed the basis of most of Britain's heavy draught breeds, the Friesian cow, which is now numerous throughout the world, and the Fries Melkschaap, a relatively scarce but high-production milking sheep.

In many parts of the world, sheep are valued more for the production of milk than either meat or wool. The Roquefort cheese industry in France is based on the milk of the Lacaune breed, while further East the Chios of Greece and Turkey and the Awassi of Israel are dominant breeds. The Fries Melkschaap has spread to several European countries while remaining a minority breed in its native area. In the Federal Republic of Germany it is outnumbered by the Oldenberg, and yet in trials in Britain the progeny of the related British Milksheep rams achieved better results than any others, with the progeny of the Oldenberg faring almost the worst.

In planning for the future, there is an urgent need to search out breeds that function most efficiently in particular circumstances. In low-input systems, the Soay, Tamworth, Shetland and similar breeds have much to offer; breeds such as the British Milksheep, Holstein and Simmental find their metier in high-output systems; while breeds such as the North Ronaldsay and the Texas Longhorn can utilise resources that might otherwise be wasted. In a world of finite resources we cannot afford wastage, and efficiency is a virtue to be encouraged.

# CHAPTER 5

# AESTHETIC APPEAL

## Religion and Recreation

For as many thousands of years as we can trace back into the history of Man, animals have been an important focus of his attention. Even before a species was domesticated it was the subject of Man's artistic skill. The life-like coloured cave paintings at Altamira and Lascaux were executed by artists who lived as long as 15,000 years ago, and since then the development of various cultures has been closely integrated with both wild and domestic livestock. Horns and colour were features of particular importance. It is probable that cattle were domesticated initially, not as suppliers of meat or milk, but as sacrificial animals in fertility rites to the lunar mother-goddess – perhaps because their lyre-shaped horns were reminiscent of the crescent moon. Throughout history the association of cattle with religion recurs. Among the Battle-Axe people and the Celts, the various colours of cattle were connected with the worship of pagan spirits: black animals symbolised pestilence and death, red animals fertility and crops, and white animals the worship of the sun.

Cattle were the currency of pre-Christian Ireland. Three ordinary cows were the price of a maidservant, but one white cow with coloured ears was worth six women slaves. In the national epic, Tain Bo Cualnge (The Cattle Raid of Cooley), mention is made of the sacrifice at Magh Ai of 300 white cows with red ears. Druid priests used white cattle in their sacrifices and may have introduced the rituals to Ireland when fleeing westwards from the Romans. The hump of Zebu cattle may also have religious significance. It has been suggested that the hump, in common with

the fat tail of some sheep breeds and the steatopygia seen in women of some African tribes, may have arisen as a result of deliberate selection rather than as a physiological adaptation to desert conditions.

Animals have been used as a source of entertainment since the earliest civilisations. The Cretan sport of bull-leaping in the second millennium BC was an artistic foretaste of the more brutal spectacle of the Roman amphitheatre or the present-day cult of the bullfight in Spain and Mexico. Since the abolition of bear-baiting and cock-fighting in the early nineteenth century, most legal British sports have been associated with horses, and these also have their roots embedded in early history. Turkmene horses, possible ancestors of the Thoroughbred, were bred for racing as early as 1000 BC. The game of polo evolved from baiga, the mounted sport par excellence, which is still played by the nomads of central Asia, as it was by their Bactrian forebears. The war chariot played a large part in popularising the horse, and chariot racing has its modern counterparts in chuck wagon racing at rodeos and sulky (trotting) racing. Special breeds, such as the Standardbred in North America and the Orloff in Russia, have been developed for trotting and pacing.

It is likely that entertainment will continue to be a significant factor in the conservation of endangered breeds, whether it be in the circus, where animals like the Spotted Pony are required to perform unusual and unnatural tricks for the amusement of those who enjoy them; in safari parks, where exotic animals are exhibited; or in farm parks, which rely on the appeal of attractive and rare breeds of domestic livestock. With the decline of agriculture in Britain, farm parks can be a viable alternative enterprise, and this was the motivation for several privately owned developments. However, the value of public amenity centres has been recognised increasingly by large organisations, such as the National Trust which owns an important farm park at Wimpole Hall near Cambridge, and by city authorities such as Leeds which has established the biggest farm park at the Temple Newsam Estate. Now farm parks have been established in other countries, and Joywind Farm Rare Breeds Conservancy in Ontario, The Institute for Agricultural Biodiversity in Iowa and Tierpark Warder in Schleswig-Holstein, have very ambitious plans. The sentiment surrounding rare breeds exerts a powerful attraction on the general public, who are intrigued by coloured sheep, longhorned cattle and massive heavy horses. Several minority breeds may have been saved from extinction because of their unusual colour or spectacular horns.

LEFT:
*Head of Dynevor Rachel 25th, a White Park cow bred by the author on his Northumberland Pennine hill farm*

ABOVE:
*Striped piglets resulting from interbreeding wild boar / Tamworth crossbred pigs*

ABOVE:
*A lamb with Soay markings, whose dam was a Welsh Half bred ewe, and sire a Down ram*

RIGHT:
*Vaynol cattle. A young bull, Allun, with Ebony and Leri*

## Colour

Among the twelve native British breeds of cattle that are dangerously low in numbers, seven have a distinctive colour pattern. The Irish Moiled, Longhorn and Gloucester have a white stripe, known as 'finching', down the back and tail, while the White Park, Vaynol and British White are all white with black or red points (muzzle, ears, eyelids, horn tips, teats and feet) and the Belted Galloway has a white belt. In all these cases the colour pattern makes it more likely that the breed will survive, even if only in farm parks. Other breeds are less fortunate. The fact that they are good, honest cattle, capable of amply rewarding a sympathetic owner, carries little weight with farm park visitors. Maybe if the Irish Dun and Suffolk Dun had been a more spectacular colour they might have escaped extinction.

Sometimes the colour of a breed can be a definite disadvantage. When progressive commercial breeders in the Midlands, and particularly Derbyshire, crossed Welsh Black cattle with the local white or roan Shorthorns in the early years of this century, neither colour was dominant, and the intermingling of black and white hairs in the coat of the progeny produced a characteristic blue roan. It was unfortunate that the breeders chose to name their new type after its colour, because the colour did not breed true. Shorthorn breeders accept red, red and white, white and red roan animals within the standards of their breed, but the Blue Albion was committed to one colour – black, black and white and white animals that were born each generation were culled. A similar situation arose with Blue Andalusian poultry, where only half the chicks are blue and the remainder, which are speckled black and white, must be removed.

Unfortunately, some very attractive colours fail to breed true. Palomino horses were kept by the priests of temples dedicated to the god Frey in pre-Christian Norway for use in processions at the seasonal festivals, and today their eye-catching colour attracts attention. However, if palomino horses are mated, half the progeny will be either chestnut or cremollo, and the most effective way to breed palominos is to mate a chestnut with a cremello horse. Similarly, in pigs, the white belt of the British Saddleback varies from an insignificant white mark on the shoulder to a belt that stretches from neck to rump, and many pigs must be culled in order to maintain the colour pattern within the standards of the breed.

Some of the ancient colours and patterns are not dominant. The greyish-brown of the wild boar is soon masked by the white colour of domestic breeds, and the patterned brown of Soay sheep is

ABOVE LEFT:
*A herd of Dairy Shorthorn cattle near Preston in Lancashire, showing the range of colours in the breed*

ABOVE:
*Shirine, a light red roan Caspian mare bred in Iran, with her foal. The breed is now almost extinct in Iran, and has been conserved mainly in Britain by the British Caspian Trust*

lost in crossing with white-woolled sheep. These colours may reappear in later generations. The horizontal camouflage stripes of wild piglets have been seen on feral pigs in New Zealand, despite their entirely domestic descent. Likewise, in a trial carried out at Ash Farm in Devon all the lambs resulting from crosses of Soay with Dorset Horn or Merino sheep were white, but when they themselves were mated to rams of Down breeds they produced some Soay-patterned lambs by a Ryeland ram, although all the lambs by a Shropshire ram were white.

Two ancient colours in horses are in vivid contrast. One is the drab colour seen in Przewalski's horse: with domestication this evolved into a range of duns, from cream through mouse to red, sometimes with a dark dorsal stripe and stripes on the forearms and gaskins, and these colours may be seen in the Highland Pony, Fjord ponies from Norway, the Sorraia, the Caspian horse, and in old, pure specimens of the Connemara Pony. The old heavy draught breeds, the Ardennes and the Belgian, are often sorrel or roan, colours related to dun. The other ancient colour probably originated with the tropical branch of the wild ancestors of the domestic horse. Spotted horses, painted in ochre and charcoal, adorn the caves at Lascaux. It is remarkable how the pattern of spots on a horse's quarters may be so close together as to give the effect of zebra stripes, and the coloured spots can be felt above the level of the silky coat, as if they were superimposed. The ancient Bactrian/Iranian legend of Sohrab and Rustum attaches great value to horses, and Rustum's choice of steed, Rakush, a spotted colt, was in colour like rose leaves scattered on a saffron ground. Spotted horses have been held in high regard for many centuries on the mainland of Europe, especially in Denmark where the Knabstrup is bred, while in North America they were drawn together in the Appaloosa Horse Club in 1938; both types originated in Spain. In Britain, spotted horses have not been paid the same respect and attention until recent times. The Romanies have probably done much to conserve this ancient colour, and a Breed Society has now been formed. Several recognised variations are known as leopard spot, polka dot, blanket, harlequin and speckled. It is possible that the spotted pattern arose naturally with domestication. It has been recorded that when the Przewalski horse is kept in zoological gardens, white marks or dark spots may appear in the coat. Similarly, some deer have a bald (white) face, and it is clear that changes in colour can appear very quickly even with partial domestication. In its very early stages in ancient Egypt, the wide range of colours recorded in cattle included red, roan, black and white, and fawn and white.

Domestic cattle are descended from one wild ancestor, the Aurochs, which seems to have been uniform in type and colour. The red colour of calves at birth turned to red–brown with a darker

neck in the adult cows, or black with a lighter stripe down the back and a mealy ring around the muzzle in the case of mature bulls. This colour pattern is closely related to the brindle pattern and can be reproduced exactly by mating together black Holstein cattle which carry the red recessive and a black-pattern gene. It has been noted also in Shetland cattle. Carissima (HB No. 38), born in 1905, was described in Volume II of the Herd Book as 'black with a brown tinge on the back and muzzle', and Cissy of Drom (HB No. 308), born in 1909, was black and white with a brown stripe down the back and a brown muzzle. Of the fifteen Shetland bulls registered in 1921, seven were dun or grey, five were black and white, and two were black with a brown muzzle and rig, known as 'rigget' in the islands.

A similar pattern can be seen more distinctly in the Telemark in Norway, the Pinzgau in Austria, the Vosgienne in France, the Longhorn in England and the Irish Moiled in Ulster. In them the finching is a broad white stripe down the length of the back, but it is only one phase in a colour pattern that has the dark mahogany colour of the Gloucester, with a white tail, at one extreme, and the white coat with coloured points, as seen in the British White and Fjall, at the other extreme. The whole range of the pattern can be demonstrated when British White cattle are crossed with other breeds. The basic white pattern is diluted progressively by crossing; colour builds up first on the neck and front limbs, and then on the sides of the body, finally to give a typical line-back pattern.

From 1921 to 1946 British White cattle were included in the same Herd Book as White Park cattle, and it was assumed by many breeders that they were simply variants of the same breed, one being polled and the other horned. However, an analysis of the colour genetics of each breed makes the distinction between them quite clear. Whereas the British White shows a gradation of overmarking as described above, the White Park is either correctly marked or black. There is no intermediate stage. Likewise, some authors have suggested that the Romans introduced the White Park cattle, and deduce from that assumption that the White Park is closely related to the Italian White breeds, such as the Chianina. Even apart from the evidence for the existence of White Park-type cattle in Ireland in pre-Roman times, they have entirely different colour patterns. The Chianina, while appearing pure porcelain white, is basically a grey animal with a black tail switch, and the calves are red–grey at birth; the colour is not dominant, and is not transmitted to crossbred progeny. In contrast, the White Park pattern is dominant, probably over any other colour. The calves are white at birth and the tail switch is white. In 1947 a white bull with black points was purchased in California and used in a herd of Holstein cows. Thirty years later, without any further introduction, there were seventy 'White Park' Holsteins in the herd. An even stronger example of the dominance

*These crossbred calves by the White Park bull, Gallangad Hector, are out of a variety of cows including Luing, Hereford, Angus and Shorthorn*

of the colour pattern is provided by the Cadzow herd in Scotland. In the early years of this century Ayrshire cows in a neighbouring dairy herd were covered by a Cadzow White Park bull. Since then the cattle have been changed from Ayrshire to Friesian and only dairy bulls have been used, yet White Park-coloured animals can still be seen in the herd.

The ability to transmit colour to the progeny varies from bull to bull. A bull that is homozygous for the White Park pattern will colour-mark any other breed. One of the outstanding bulls, Whipsnade 281, was mated to several breeds of cow, including Longhorn, Belted Galloway and Welsh Black, but he passed on his colour to all his progeny. Some of his sons, such as Gallangad Hector, are also homozygous for the correct colour pattern, but others, such as Royal Beast, throw a proportion of black calves. Of the calves from another heterozygous bull mated to Friesian cows, half were correctly marked and half were black. Similar matings of hererozygous White Park cows with a Hereford bull produced twelve calves, of which six were white with black or red points, five were black with a white head, and one was red with a white head.

The White Park colour pattern is associated with the Hamitic Longhorn, which spread into Africa about 4000 BC. From there it reached Spain (where many Berrenda and Cardena cattle are of the same colour), north-western Europe and, at a later date, the Americas, where the Blanco Orejinegro and some specimens of the Texas Longhorn are similarly marked. Other branches of the Hamitic Longhorn carried related colours deeper into Africa where they are found in the Fulani cattle of Nigeria and the Nguni cattle of Zululand. The Nguni cattle were divided into herds according to colour by the great Zulu leader, Chaka, and each colour was given a name. The six basic colours, white, black, brown, red, dun and yellow, were further divided into seven distinct patterns. The white cattle with black points comprising the royal herd were known as Nhlophekati, while the line-backed animals resembling the Telemark or Witrik were known as Nkoni. Cattle of an intermediate flecked or spotted pattern were prized highly, as the hides were valued for covering the warriors' shields.

Colour has long played an important role in aesthetic aspects of livestock breeding, but it may well be associated also with commercial factors. Apart from the well-documented value of colour-marking in breeds such as the Hereford and White Park, it has been shown, for example, that coloured Icelandic sheep are more prolific than their white flockmates, and that black Leicester sheep produce a lean carcass of superior quality to white Leicesters. In other cases colour is associated with genetic defects and with lethal genes. In a strain of heterozygous yellow laboratory mice,

RIGHT:
*Texas Longhorn steer aged 17 years*

BELOW RIGHT:
*A 22 year-old Texas Longhorn cow that never failed to wean a good calf*

the foetuses which are homozygous for yellow die at an early stage of gestation. Similar conditions are known in platinum foxes, albino horses, and some grey sheep. In other cases, colour is associated with a reduction in vigour or lack of development. White heifers of some breeds have under-development of the uterus, cervix and anterior vagina, and are incapable of breeding. The condition is found in about 10 per cent of white Shorthorn heifers in Great Britain, and also in some foreign breeds. Among Soay sheep a small proportion are light in colour and without the moufflon pattern (i.e. tan self-coloured), and they have a higher mortality and lower growth rate than animals of other colours within the breed.

## Horns

It has been generally accepted that the absence or presence of horns is controlled by one pair of genes, that polledness is dominant to hornedness, and that the multihorned character in sheep is dominant to the normal two horns. In reality the genetics of horns are much more complex.

Sheep breeders in Australia produced the Poll Dorset by crossing their Dorset Horn ewes with Ryeland rams. The progeny were then back-crossed to Dorset Horn rams, but only the polled

progeny in each generation were retained, until polled animals true to the Dorset type were produced. If polledness is dominant to hornedness, this programme would not necessarily eliminate
the 'horn' genes. They might by chance be passed from generation to generation in a recessive state
to reappear in the future. The pedigree of the horned ewe, Colerne L608 provides an example of
this, as one grandparent, S44, was horned:

|  | Sire H321 (polled) | Grandsire D110 (polled) |
|  |  | Granddam W265 (polled) |
| L608 (horned) |  |  |
|  | Dam F203 (polled) | Grandsire D110 (polled) |
|  |  | Granddam S44 (horned) |

If this theory is correct, the reverse should not occur, but in my own flock the polled ewe, Colerne
J470, had only one polled grandparent:

|  | Sire F202 (horned) | Grandsire D110 (polled) |
|  |  | Granddam S44 (horned) |
| J470 (polled) |  |  |
|  | Dam F 131 (horned) | Grandsire A138 (horned) |
|  |  | Granddam Z183 (horned) |

The inheritance of horns is more complicated in sheep than it is in cattle. In some breeds, such
as the black-faced hill sheep, Whitefaced Woodland, Wiltshire Horn and Portland, both sexes are
horned. In the longwool and Down breeds both sexes are polled, but between these two extremes
are many combinations from horned rams with some polled females to all polled females with
some horned rams. Sometimes the true position is obscured by artificial selection. On the island of
Hirta about 46 per cent of Soay ewes are horned, but on the mainland almost all Soay females are
horned. This was dictated by fashion.

In cattle, the strength of the genetic factor for horns seems to vary from breed to breed. Although polledness is generally dominant, a cross between a strongly horned breed, such as the
Longhorn, and a weakly polled breed, such as the Aberdeen Angus or British White, might produce horned offspring, whereas the Galloway, which is strongly polled, can be expected to produce only polled offspring when it is crossed with other breeds.

The long spectacular horns of the Longhorn, which once almost led to its extinction because
they prevented close stocking in yards, are now a major part of its attraction in farm parks. A
controversy which developed within the Longhorn Cattle Society arose from the desire of some
members to keep polled Longhorn for use in commercial units. White Park cattle are also found in
farm parks, partly on account of their horns, but the largest recorded pair of White Park horns,
found on a Dynevor bullock and measuring 153 cm from tip to tip, bears no comparison with the
horns of the Aurochs. The Aurochs stood almost 2 m high at the shoulder, and often measured
305–335 cm from horn tip to horn tip. A horn converted into a drinking goblet and measuring 200
cm long was in existence until about 150 years ago. Among domesticated cattle, the most notable
heads are found in the Texas Longhorn breed. 'Champion', a famous steer calved by the Rio
Grande in 1890, was exhibited at fairs and shows throughout North America. In his prime he
weighed only 544 kg, but the circumference of each horn was 45 cm at the base, and the distance
from horn tip to horn tip was 263 cm (although 292 cm was the span claimed). Other unsubstan-
tiated reports speak of horns up to 413 cm tip to tip.

The heads of sheep can be equally showy. The single pair of horns which suffice for most breeds
may vary from the smooth curve of Soay horns to the impressive spirals of the Portland, and from
the light, rounded horns of Shetland rams to the sharp-edged, corrugated horns of the North
Ronaldsay, but to the general public two horns in sheep are not very exciting. The appeal of
Longhorn cattle horns, however, is matched by the eye-catching nature of several pairs of horns in
sheep. It is likely that the multihorned factor arose spontaneously in different populations. It occurs
widely, from the Middle East and North Africa to the Hebrides and Iceland. It is still found in the
Shetland Islands, and used to be found in Spain, which is doubtless the origin of the multihorned
sheep herded by the Navajo Indians in New Mexico. The inheritance of the multihorned character-

ABOVE:
*Two Longhorn steers*

ABOVE CENTRE:
*A 4-horned Uruguayan ram, probably descended from sheep imported from Spain, and thus may be related distantly to the Jacob*

ABOVE RIGHT:
*The skull of a 4-horned sheep showing how the bones may fail to knit together*

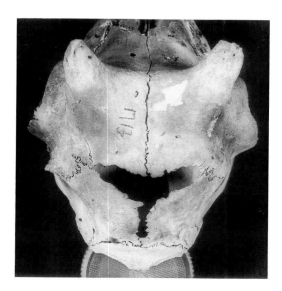

istic is controlled at two loci and it is not a staightforward dominant/recessive mechanism. Theoretically, it is possible to breed either true-breeding four-horned or true-breeding two-horned sheep, but in practice this would be very difficult. Hebridean breeders have tended to favour two-horned sheep in recent years, but the 1991 census of Manx Loghtan breeding ewes showed that c.60% were two-horned, and the others were multihorned or polled.

| Sire and Dam | % progeny with | |
|---|---|---|
| | 2 horns | 2+ horns/polled |
| All 4-horned | 34.0 | 66.0 |
| All 2-horned | 93.5 | 6.5 |

Of the three multihorned British breeds, the Hebridean and the Manx Loghtan clearly have the same origin, but the Jacob probably owes more of its ancestry to Spanish sheep. It is appreciably larger, has a long tail, and its colour pattern is quite distinctive. In all these breeds four horns were favoured. The largest horns grow upwards from the top of the head, and sometimes incline forwards to such a degree in rams that the animal is unable to graze. The lower pair grows from the sides of the head, in some cases curling round to grow into the face. The horn shape appears to be highly heritable, and careful selection of breeding rams should be exercised to avoid problems. In flocks where four-horned ewes and rams have been used exclusively, the horns have often deteriorated in quality, becoming weak and deformed. In addition, the horn buds of four-horned lambs are very easily damaged, and the bones of the skull may not fuse properly in four-horned sheep. The use of two-horned rams will produce stronger horns in their progeny, and many of the rams with good four-horned heads have one two-horned parent. Some Hebridean and Manx Loghtan ewes are polled, with a pronounced growth of wool on the forehead. These animals behave genetically as if they were multihorned.

## Wool

It is significant that all three multihorned British breeds of sheep also have coloured wool, which provides a second attractive characteristic in the same animal and increases its visual novelty. In recent years, there has been a strong renewal of interest in hand spinning and weaving, and the demand for naturally coloured wool now far exceeds the supply. The return to cottage industry is

*A flock of Hebridean sheep in the Lake District c.1900. A high proportion of the ewes are polled with a prominent tuft of wool on the forehead and behave genetically as 4-horned sheep*

not confined to the British Isles. The Navajo Indians have long had a coloured-wool industry. The white Texel flocks in Holland are dotted with black sheep whose wool supplies a growing market, while the recently formed Coloured Sheep Associations in several countries, result from the increasing international demand for coloured wool. A five-yearly World Congress on Coloured Sheep has been held in Adelaide, Australia (1979), New Zealand (1984) and Oregon, USA (1989). The next Congress will be held in York, UK in 1994. Australia has no coloured breeds of sheep, but 164 rams were registered in Volume II of the Flock Book of the South Australian Coloured Sheep Owners' Society Inc. A few of these rams showed the 'badger' (or 'reversed badger') pattern, and these arose mainly from Border Leicester foundation stock. Some were spotted, and these owed most of their ancestry to the Merino, but the majority of the rams were whole-coloured, mainly black, and were derived from a variety of white breeds, generally of longwool type. Black is usually a recessive factor, as in the case of the Hebridean whose crossbred progeny out of white ewes are usually white. However, the Black Welsh Mountain and the Jacob carry a gene for dominant black, so that their crossbred progeny usually are black, except in the case of Jacob crosses with the Dorset Horn and other pink-nosed breeds, when the spotted colour may persist. It used to be considered an ill omen to have black lambs in a flock, rather as misfortune was associated with black calves in herds of White Park cattle. On the other hand, black wool was commonly applied as a cure for earache until the seventeenth century, and the royal physicians advised George III to wear black woollen stockings to cure his rheumatism.

Wool is required by hand spinners and weavers for several purposes. The white Wensleydale fleece, too harsh for spinning into knitting wool, was traditionally used for jacket linings, but its high lustre and strength make it an ideal thread for tapestry work. Recently, the Wensleydale Flock Book has included a black section as 15–20 per cent of the lambs born in this breed are black. The most common use of wool in the cottage industry is for the production of knitting and crochet wool, for weaving dress and furnishing fabrics, and for rug making. In addition, there are specialist requirements, such as the manufacture of sheepskin products, for which the Lincoln Longwool is in great demand. The wool for knitting and crochet work may be considered as one type, which must be fine, with a quality of 50–58 and a fibre length of 7.5–15 cm. The quality number, referred to as the Bradford Count, indicates the number of hanks into which a pound of wool could theoretically be spun – the higher the rating, the finer the wool. Crimp is desirable, especially for lightweight woollens, but is not required where wool is spun without carding. Kemp fibres do not absorb dye and are therefore not an asset in wool that is to be coloured artificially, unless such an effect is deliberately sought.

Wool dyeing is an ancient craft. More than 3000 years ago, an industry based on the purple dye extracted from a shellfish, murex, was developed on a large scale on the Phoenician coast, where there was a major trading fleet by 1000 BC. The development of the dyeing industry was associated with an increased demand for white wool provided by the sheep of Greece and Anatolia. The convex heads of these sheep, heavy-horned like the Merino, were portrayed on ancient coins from Asia Minor. Natural colour in a fleece is an advantage, however, as it eliminates the necessity for dyeing, a process that removes the natural oils from the wool, making it less waterproof. Breeds which yield fleeces suitable for the production of knitting wool include the Portland for white wool, while the Shetland and the Hebridean are pre-eminent among the coloured breeds.

The next category of wool products covers a relatively wide range of items including worsted cloths, tweeds, dress fabrics, hosiery and knee rugs. The strength of the wool fibres is more important than their softness. Crimp, colour and lustre are factors of high priority, while kemp is again undesirable, except in the production of tweeds which derive much of their character from these thick, white fibres. The staple length should be 10–20 cm and the Bradford Count 44–54. The Whitefaced Woodland and Derbyshire Gritstone provide suitable wool in this category, while the Border Leicester and British Milksheep have the added advantage of lustre. Extremely attractive

BREED OF THE ZETLAND AND ORKNEY ISLANDS.

*A ewe and ram from the Orkney Islands in the early nineteenth century, showing the type from which the Shetland breed developed, from a painting by William Shiels, R.S.A.*

worsted materials in shades of moorit (red-brown) can be produced from the wool of the Manx Loghtan, although in theory the fibres are rather short for this purpose.

The finest wool obtained from domestic sheep comes from the Merino, and its quality is the end-product of centuries of selective breeding programmes. The average fibre diameter of Merino wool is about 22.5 microns, whereas the coarser longwool fibres from the fleece of a breed such as the Cotswold has an average diameter of about 45 microns. However, it is interesting to compare Merino wool with that of ancient or wild sheep. The wool fibres in a Soay fleece are almost as fine as those of the Merino, while wool used to weave cloth found in a Scythian tomb in the Crimea, which dates from the fifth century BC, had an average diameter of only 15 microns. Relics of the ancient Anatolian finewool sheep can be found in the Dubrovnik and Chalkidiki breeds of Yugoslavia and Greece. It would seem that selection has not produced finer wool. The finest fibres are found in the undercoat of the wild Moufflon: it has an average diameter of only 12 microns, little more than half the width of Merino wool fibres.

The study of the genetics of wool colour starts with the Soay. On Hirta about 67½ per cent of the Soay sheep are chocolate in colour; with buff markings over the eyes, on the bottom jaw, the rump patch and the belly; about 22½ per cent are fawn with the same pattern; about 5 per cent are self-coloured (i.e. without pattern); and about 5 per cent have white markings; a few are black. Chocolate is dominant to fawn, and the pattern is dominant to self-colour; however, the pattern is recessive to white, because it occasionally reappears among lambs in flocks of white sheep. When this happens it can often be traced back to a source in Welsh Mountain sheep. The link between the breeds is demonstrated by the Torddu and Torwen varieties of Welsh sheep. The Torwen has white, pale grey or tan markings on a dark background in the same pattern as the Soay; the Torddu has the pattern in reverse as does the Barbados Blackbelly. The Castlemilk Moorit also has the same colouring and pattern as the Soay. The Soay fleece consists of very fine underwool mixed with a variable proportion of strong hairs, and is normally shed naturally.

As sheep were increasingly subjected to artificial selection, the range of colours widened and the proportion of white fibres increased. Among the North Ronaldsay sheep on Linga Holm in 1979, eight separate colours were identified by Pilkington. When selecting rams for this flock, a higher proportion of black and moorit animals are retained to reduce the chance of these recessive colours being eliminated.

*A flock of Gotland sheep at Gallangad Farm near Loch Lomond in 1977. The breed was imported from Sweden in 1972 by Mr and Mrs W.F. Macdonald*

*The Colours of Sheep on the Island of Linga Holm in 1979 expressed as a percentage*

| Colour | Ewes | Rams |
|---|---|---|
| White | 26.3 | 16(4) |
| Light grey | 26.7 | 36(9) |
| Medium grey | 15.2 | 16(4) |
| Dark grey | 18.9 | 16(4) |
| Parti-coloured | 1.0 | 4(1) |
| Roan | 4.2 | −(−) |
| Black | 7.4 | 4(1) |
| Moorit | 0.5 | 8(2) |

The next step in the improvement of wool on British breeds can be seen in the Shetland. The wool is the finest produced by any native British sheep, with a quality of up to 60, and formed the basis of the world-famous Shetland woollen industry. Shetland shawls are so fine and soft that they can be drawn through a wedding ring, and the multicoloured Fair Isle sweaters are knitted in natural colours to traditional patterns that have been passed down from generation to generation as the property of individual families. The various colours of Shetland wool are more clearly defined than those of the North Ronaldsay. White is dominant, followed by grey, black and moorit, although there are other patterns and variations. The recessive colour, moorit, always breeds true. Some colours are known by Shetland dialect names, and these are derived from Old Norse words. Thus dark grey is shaela (from ON hela = hoar frost), brown is moorit (ON moraudr = peat brown), and a blaze is snedled (ON snudr = snout or muzzle). Emsket is blue–grey, while katmoget sheep have a light-coloured body with a dark belly and legs and patterned face like the Torddu. In earlier times, Shetland sheep were rooed (plucked) in a gradual process which was carried out as the wool reached a fit state at different times on different parts of the body. The soft wool was removed, leaving behind the stronger fibres to provide the sheep with some measure of protection. Grey wool, in particular, is a combination of fine white and coarse black fibres.

Within the grey category of fleece is a type which can be described as blue. It consists of a mixture of white and black fibres, but in this case all the fibres are fine. The combination of fineness, softness, colour and lustre in wool of this type makes it particularly desirable. A closely related breed, originating on the island of Gotland in the Baltic, owes its present popularity to this

## Characteristics of the Wool of Some British Breeds of Sheep

| Category | Breed | Quality | Staple length (cm) | Notes |
|---|---|---|---|---|
| MOUNTAIN (*coarse wool*) | Scottish Blackface | 28–32 | 20–30 | |
| | Rough Fell | 28–32 | 20–30 | |
| | Herdwick | 28–32 | 15–20 | |
| | Swaledale | 32–40 | 15–20 | |
| | Dalesbred | 32–40 | 15–25 | |
| MEDIUM WOOL | Welsh Mountain | 36–48 | 5–15 | Variable in quality |
| | Soay | 44–50 | 5–8 | Brown |
| | Devon Closewool | 46–50 | 8–10 | |
| | Black Welsh Mountain | 44–52 | 8–10 | Dominant Black |
| | Manx Loghtan | 44–52 | 8–10 | Moorit |
| | Jacob | 44–52 | 10–15 | Spotted |
| | Hebridean | 48–52 | 10–15 | Black or dark brown |
| | Lonk | 46–54 | 10–15 | |
| | Whitefaced Woodland | 48–54 | 10–20 | |
| | Exmoor Horn | 48–56 | 8–12 | |
| | Radnor | 48–56 | 8–15 | |
| | Derbyshire Gritstone | 48–56 | 13–18 | |
| | North Ronaldsay | 50–56 | 5–10 | Various colours |
| | Portland | 50–56 | 6–9 | Red at birth |
| | Cheviot (all types) | 50–56 | 8–10 | |
| | Oxford Down | 50–56 | 10–15 | |
| SHORTWOOL AND DOWN (*fine wool*) | Shropshire | 54–56 | 10–15 | |
| | Kerry Hill | 54–56 | 8–15 | |
| | Suffolk | 54–58 | 8–10 | |
| | Dorset Horn | 54–58 | 8–10 | |
| | Clun Forest | 54–58 | 8–10 | |
| | Llanwenog | 54–58 | 6–10 | |
| | Dorset Down | 56–58 | 5–10 | |
| | Hampshire Down | 56–58 | 5–10 | |
| | Ryeland | 56–58 | 5–10 | Badger faced pattern recessive |
| | Southdown | 56–60 | 4–6 | |
| | Shetland | 56–60 | 5–15 | Various colours |
| LONGWOOL AND LUSTRE | Devon and Cornwall Longwool | 32–40 | 20–30 | |
| | Whitefaced Dartmoor | 36–40 | 20–25 | |
| | Dartmoor Greyface | 36–40 | 20–25 | |
| | Lincoln Longwool | 36–44 | 25–35 | Broad staple |
| | Cotswold | 40–44 | 15–25 | |
| | Leicester Longwool | 40–46 | 20–30 | Black recessive |
| | Teeswater | 40–48 | 25–30 | |
| | Wensleydale | 44–48 | 25–35 | High degree of purl and lustre |
| | Border Leicester | 44–50 | 15–25 | |
| | British Milksheep | 48–56 | 15–20 | |
| | Romney Marsh | 48–56 | 15–20 | |

type of wool, which has been developed specially for the production of grey sheepskin coats. The programme has been so successful that the Gotland is now the most common breed in Sweden.

In contrast, breeders of Shetland sheep were influenced more by the prices obtainable from the British Wool Marketing Board, which discriminated severely against non-white wool, paying 25 per cent less than for white wool of the same quality. Although the Shetland Islands did not fall within the jurisdiction of the Board, its emphasis on white wool resulted in the rapid decline in the numbers of non-white Shetland sheep. In some cases Cheviot rams were introduced, and the evidence of such crosses is still seen in some sheep which are larger and have a longer tail. Although there are many thousands of sheep on the Islands which are described as Shetlands, a high proportion are not pure, and even among those that can claim an unquestionable pedigree the majority are white. Pure-bred, coloured Shetland sheep reached very low numbers and could very easily have become extinct but for the revived interest in hand spinning, and the publicity given by organisations such as the Rare Breeds Survival Trust and the Combined Flock Book, which together gave the Shetland breed a new respectability and a more secure future. In 1986 the Rare Breeds Survival Trust achieved a significant concession from the British Wool Marketing Board. There is a statutory requirement that all wool from producers with four or more sheep must be sold to, or through, the Board, but under the new arrangement rare breeds from the three highest catagories in the Priority List (Critical, Endangered, Vulnerable) have been given exemption from this requirement to allow producers to market their wool 'direct to a user for the purpose of handspinning by that user'.

# CHAPTER 6

# COMMERCIAL CONSIDERATIONS

# Efficient Production

More than a hundred years ago, Victorian farmers undertook an enlightened series of experiments to compare various breeds of sheep. The trials, carried out by members of the Partington Tenants' Club in Yorkshire in 1862, were intended to measure efficiency of production in relation to profitability. The cost of the feedstuffs consumed by the sheep was deducted from the value of the mutton and wool produced, and the groups were ranked in order of the cash surplus achieved. Seven breeds or types of sheep, each represented by six animals were included in the trials; five of them are now numerically small and endangered in their country of origin. The most profitable turned out to be the Lincoln and the Shropshire Down, both now minority breeds.

*Comparative Sheep Trials 11 November 1861–14 February 1862*

| Breed | Carcass increase | | Wool yield | | Value of output | Cost of feed | Margin |
|---|---|---|---|---|---|---|---|
| | weight | value | weight | value | | | |
| | kg | £ | kg | £ | £ | £ | £ |
| Lincoln | 67 | 3.52 | 140 | 1.65 | 5.17 | 3.65 | 1.52 |
| Shropshire Down | 63 | 3.59 | 90 | 1.03 | 4.62 | 3.33 | 1.29 |
| Leicester | 62 | 3.26 | 94 | 1.10 | 4.36 | 3.23 | 1.13 |
| South Down | 51 | 3.03 | 59 | 0.66 | 3.69 | 2.83 | 0.86 |
| Cotswold | 49 | 2.72 | 114 | 1.35 | 4.07 | 3.33 | 0.74 |
| North Sheep | 52 | 2.88 | 93 | 1.06 | 3.94 | 3.31 | 0.63 |
| Teeswater cross | 54 | 2.95 | 91 | 1.08 | 4.03 | 3.44 | 0.59 |

Once again, the importance of relating output to input has been understood more clearly in recent years, but in the long interval between the Partington experiments and present-day developments, livestock selection and management systems were directed towards high production, almost irrespective of cost. Milking competitions and laying trials used milk yields in a specified period or the annual hen-housed average as the measure of comparison. The National Lambing Competition counted only the number of lambs reared, without regard for the size of the ewe or the standard of management. The Meat and Livestock Commission gave high priority to intensive stocking rates, mindless of the associated higher capital costs and greater management problems.

Perhaps the characteristic worst affected by this emphasis on total production was growth rate. When the Bull Performance Test was first introduced in Britain, bulls were ranked according to their daily weight gain on test. In itself this was an inefficient method of evaluation, as it took no account of compensatory growth patterns, but even more seriously it gave no consideration to the efficiency of feed conversion or to the production of quality meat. The obsession with growth rate resulted in various undesirable side-effects, of which the most important were an increase in the incidence of calving difficulties and a much higher calf mortality – defects accompanying the use of those breeds, particularly from continental Europe, which were becoming popular with all the publicity given to high growth rates. Comparative trials carried out in South Africa with Nguni cattle confirmed this opinion, and work in Britain has shown that breeds such as the White Park and Longhorn experience minimal problems at calving, either in pure-breeding or crossbreeding. This is partly due to their conformation, and in sheep it has been found that the primitive breeds, which have the largest pelvic dimensions relative to body size, also have the greatest ease of parturition. If relative growth rate (i.e. growth rate in relation to weight) had been used as the basis of selection, rather than absolute growth rate, these problems could have been avoided, and the native and minority breeds would have compared more favourably.

Breeding methods in the twentieth century are therefore open to criticism on two points: first, they have not been scientifically valid; and second, the improvement in major production characteristics has been partly negated by the related deterioration in other important qualities. The Milk

OPPOSITE:
*Irish Moiled bull, Laurelgrange Lawrence, at three months of age. He was bred by Mrs P. Warnock in Northern Ireland and purchased by the Rare Breeds Survival Trust*

Marketing Board found it necessary to make radical changes in the contemporary comparison system, in which the value of dairy bulls is assessed by the milk yield of their daughters, because the rating of individual bulls fluctuated so dramatically. Okery Mark, once a popular bull on the Board's élite list, achieved a result of +330 kg until 1972, when his rating plunged to −38 kg. A bull's assessment is also based on the butter-fat percentage of his daughters' milk, but it is questionable whether high butter-fat is desirable in view of its possible association with coronary heart disease and other disorders. The same criticism can be levelled at some modern methods of fattening farm animals. The carcass fat produced by animals fed mainly on cereal compares badly with that of breeds which subsist largely on grass and forage crops, which is rich in polyunsaturated fats. Carcass fat from intensively reared animals is not only potentially harmful, it is also more expensive to produce.

In contrast, pig-breeding methods with the popular breeds have resulted in lean carcasses, but the process has been taken to such extremes that the associated problems of pale muscle with a high moisture content, weakness in the legs, and a nervous disposition that is highly susceptible to stress, have become serious limiting factors within the pig industry. Unreliable temperament in cattle has also become more widespread. This is partly due to the increasing use of artificial insemination, where there is less opportunity to identify bulls with poor temperament, and partly to the introduction of continental breeds, which are more nervous and unpredictable. In a recent trial, the docility of White Park crossbred calves was particularly noticeable compared with the nervousness of their contemporaries sired by Limousin and Blonde d'Acquitaine bulls.

There is little doubt that modern breeds, and especially imported breeds, have a tendency to be more delicate and prone to disease, and the loss within the British sheep industry, for example, that can be attributed to mortality is estimated at more than 10 per cent of adult stock and more than 20 per cent of lambs. In comparative trials carried out by government agencies or by commercial companies, rare breeds often are not shown to best advantage as the trials are based on standards and systems to which the popular breeds are adapted. For example, in pig trials which use high-protein ad lib diets and slaughter at a high weight, rare breeds are not able to express their true value and little attention is paid to genotype-environment interactions in which rare breeds of several species compare very favourably in more extensive lower-input systems of production. Comparative trials in the Scottish uplands during the late 1980s showed that crossbred lambs by the Bleu du Maine and Rouge de l'Ouest had a high mortality rate, while their contemporaries sired by British Milksheep rams were strong survivors. In an effort to combat such losses the

*White Park cow and calf: The distinctive markings, which generally are black but occasionally red, are normally found on the muzzle, eyelids, ears, teats and forefeet. The tips of the horns are black*

farming industry has used an increasing volume of vaccines to control disease, drugs to boost performance, and hormones to enable subfertile stock to perpetuate its deficiencies. It has also intensified livestock enterprises, sometimes to an unacceptable level, and this has served to exacerbate the problems.

If these are the achievements of livestock breeding and improvement in the twentieth century, the recent return to principles established by the Partington Tenants' Club is a timely and welcome relief for those breeds which have been pushed aside in the last hundred or even fifty years. The change of heart was prompted partly by the adoption of a performance registry for some breeds: for example, the Red Angus breed in North America set a basic standard of 215 kg at 205 days for bulls before they can be registered, while in Britain all British Milksheep ewes must be recorded to qualify for registration, and rams must be progeny-tested. But it was mainly the comparative sheep trials carried out by a private consultancy firm, Livestock Improvement Services, commencing in 1958, that re-established efficiency rather than the total amount of production as a priority. These trials used as a measure the amount of feed eaten by one hundred Scottish Halfbred ewes, so that the weight of lamb produced by each breed could be related to a constant input.

Other organisations followed with comparative studies, with the result that breeds which had been disregarded by the majority of commercial farmers for many decades showed themselves in many cases to be more efficient than the more popular breeds. Calves sired by White Park bulls achieved a growth rate 4½ per cent greater than that of Limousin crossbred calves out of the same group of cows, and in another trial the crossbred calves sired by a White Park bull were much heavier than their contemporaries sired by Hereford and Welsh Black bulls at 18 months of age. Likewise, Shetland ewes outperformed their Scottish Blackface flockmates as pure-breds on hill land, and under crossbreeding systems in the lowlands. When both were mated to Poll Dorset rams, twin lambs from Scottish Blackface ewes (55 kg liveweight) weighed 29.8 kg at 100 days of age, while those from Shetland ewes (32.7 kg liveweight) weighed 24.4 kg at the same age.

The value of the smaller rare breeds of sheep lies in crossbreeding systems. As pure-breds they are relatively inefficient in most circumstances. Both the Hebridean and the Shetland are less productive than the larger Whitefaced Woodland, and this would suggest that the latter breed is superior to the Scottish Blackface, taking a line of comparison through the Shetland, which was superior to the Scottish Blackface in trials carried out by the North of Scotland College of Agriculture.

Among the small endangered breeds, the Hebridean has the highest prolificacy and the highest efficiency of milk production. Measured as the weight of lamb produced in relation to the meta-

*Hebridean ram lamb with 6 horns at Ash Farm in 1974; the side horns are partially fused*

bolic weight of the ewe, its efficiency of production is also superior to that of the Shetland which is no longer a rare breed. Among the larger breeds, the Whitefaced Woodland is superior to other endangered breeds, such as the Norfolk Horn and the Wiltshire Horn.

*Comparative Performance results for Four Purebred Rare Breeds of Sheep on the same Farm (1979–86 inclusive)*

| Breed | Adult ewe wt (kg) | Gestation days | A.L.S. | Av Corrected 50 day wt (twins)(kg) | Av Corrected 100 day wt (twins)(kg) | Efficiency of production index |
|---|---|---|---|---|---|---|
| Hebridean | 36 | 148.1 | 143.97 | 26.31 | 41.10 | 4.44 |
| Manx Loghtan | 40 | 147.1 | 124.14 | 26.82 | 39.90 | 3.62 |
| Portland | 43 | 146.8 | 100.91 | 28.22 | 41.91 | 3.18 |
| Whitefaced Woodland | 61 | 149.0 | 153.54 | 40.93 | 61.26 | 4.66 |

This trial was carried out on one farm and included several breeds. Among the smaller breeds, the Hebridean, and the Manx Loghtan to a lesser degree, were better milking ewes than the Shetland, with better 50-day lamb weights. Among the larger breeds, the Whitefaced Woodland, and the Norfolk Horn to a lesser extent, were better milking ewes than the Wiltshire Horn. However, within each group the Shetland and the Wiltshire Horn lambs made better compensatory growth between 50 and 100 days of age.

*Lambing per cent of some Rare Breeds of Sheep (1991)*

| Breed | No. of ewes | Lambing % reared pure-breeding | Lambing % reared Cross-breeding |
|---|---|---|---|
| Hebridean | 817 | 146.7 | |
| Manx Loghtan | 705 | 137.4 | 156.5 |
| Soay | 450 | 135.8 | 148.9 |
| Portland | 513 | 93.2 | |

These performance figures calculated from the annual returns to the Combined Flock Book for four breeds confirm the results for comparative performance from other sources, and also demonstrate the remarkable extra prolificacy that is obtained with crossbreeding.

When small ewes of primitive breeds are mated to rams of larger meat breeds they become relatively more efficient. Trials conducted by the Rare Breeds Survival Trust, to compare a primitive breed (Hebridean) and a longwool breed (Cotswold) with the commercially popular Mule ewe, showed the Hebridean to be the most productive when mated to a meat sire.

*Comparative Efficiency of Production of Hebridean, Cotswold and Mule ewes when mated to meat breed rams*

| Ram Breed | Ewe Breed | No. of ewes per unit feed | Lambing % | Wt of twins 100 days (kg) | Index of efficiency |
|---|---|---|---|---|---|
| Hampshire Down | Hebridean | 34.8 | 156 | 21.9 | 120 |
| Hampshire Down | Mule | 20 | 174 | 29.4 | 100 |
| Suffolk | Mule | 20 | 167 | 36.2 | 100 |
| Suffolk | Cotswold | 18.9 | 129 | 33.0 | 72 |

Clearly there is ample opportunity for breeds which have avoided the pitfalls of intensification and retained the qualities that were more highly valued in earlier times to rediscover a role within the contemporary livestock industry. They can reduce loss and increase efficiency, injecting a new sense of purpose into some of the less successful enterprises.

We must be careful not to overstate the case. There is an enormous fund of variation within some popular breeds, and sometimes it may be more effective to make use of the scope this offers for selection than to turn to a minor breed. We need to recognise that each and every breed possesses distinctive characteristics. This reinforces one of the basic concepts in the conservation of minority breeds, that they must be conserved for their own particular, often unique, qualities, and for their value in crossbreeding programmes. What peculiar qualities do the minor breeds offer to justify conserving the proliferation of breeds that exist? Clearly their qualities vary from breed to breed, but a few are of extra importance.

Longevity, disease resistance, ease of parturition and quality meat production are four qualities that have been sadly neglected in recent decades. Selection for early maturity has inadvertently selected also for a shorter productive life, and the value of such long-lived breeds as Texas Longhorn and White Park cattle and Hebridean sheep has risen accordingly. Among pig breeds, the Large Black boar, Eaglethorpe Malcolm (born February 1981) and the Berkshire boar, Gillhouse Peter Lad 3 (born 2nd February 1982), were still alive and active in early 1992. The scientific explanation of disease resistance is open to some dispute, but the resistance of Soay sheep to footrot is well documented, and is in marked contrast to the delicacy of some popular modern breeds. The primitive breeds of sheep and Shetland, White Park and Longhorn cattle are noted for their ease of parturition. The tendency among the more popular British breeds to produce an overfat carcass is the consequence of the great influence exerted by the export trade from 1850 to 1950, and the value of some minority breeds will stem from their lean carcasses, either lightweight from the Hebridean or Soay, or heavyweight from the Oxford Down or Wensleydale. This may be combined in some cases with their ability to utilise a diet in a way that enhances the content of polyunsaturated fat in the carcass. Some commercial British breeds such as the British Milksheep, or imported breeds such as the Charollais, also produce high-quality lean carcasses, but this does not devalue the potential contribution of the minor sheep breeds. The results of trials carried out by the AFRC demonstrated the potential use of primitive breeds of sheep in the production of lean carcasses and the high meat quality of rare pig breeds.

*Carcass Composition of Four Breeds of Sheep*

| Breed | Soay | Hebridean | Leicester | Southdown |
|---|---|---|---|---|
| Standard slaughter weight females (kg) | 12.70 | 18.30 | 41.40 | 27.50 |
| % lean in carcass | 56.71 | 58.16 | 53.39 | 52.64 |
| % subcutaneous fat | 6.47 | 7.12 | 11.00 | 13.00 |
| % intra-muscular fat | 15.47 | 14.07 | 16.89 | 19.43 |
| % KKCF | 4.56 | 3.49 | 2.80 | 3.73 |

Hardiness is a notoriously difficult characteristic to define, but in general it denotes the ability to tolerate adverse climatic conditions. The survival of the Nguni cattle on acid pastures in the high-rainfall area of Zululand, or the superiority of Brahman cattle in a hot, tropical climate are examples of hardiness, while in Britain the attribute is related mainly to cold and wet conditions. It might reflect the specialised abilities demonstrated by North Ronaldsay sheep on the exposed shorelines of the Orkney Islands, or, among cattle, the adaptation of such breeds as the Galloway to cold, wet winds.

Thriftiness, closely associated with hardiness, is a quality of many minority breeds, including Kerry and Shetland cattle, Hebridean and Manx Loghtan sheep, and Tamworth and Gloucester Old Spots pigs. It implies the ability to survive and thrive on lower levels of nutrition in terms of both quality and quantity, which is in turn a major factor affecting efficiency of production. Rising costs and shrinking margins in pig production are renewing the recognition among breeders of the pig's traditional scavenging role. Breeds which will live happily out of doors in systems based on cheap buildings and by-product feeds are once again proving the financial advantages of a longer and less intensive production cycle.

When the special qualities and advantages of various breeds have been identified and defined, and even when their undoubted value in special environments and particular systems of production have been demonstrated, the most difficult obstacle still remains. Marketing will be the key to the successful conservation of many breeds, and it is the basic factor in the commercial equation. In the absence of an effective marketing strategy, the value of rare breeds will languish unrecognised and they will rely indefinitely on the support of external agencies for their survival.

Several useful precedents have been established. In Britain, Heal Farm (Quality Traditional Meats) is a well-established business based on rare breeds and traditional recipes, and others have been encouraged to follow this example. In France, a breeder of endangered Basque pigs has a similar business, Aldude, which has developed a market for speciality meats produced exclusively from this breed. Likewise in Spain, 'jabugo' is produced exclusively from the meat of Iberic pigs. Both Basque and Iberic pigs have special and particular characteristics not shared by other breeds, and the fashionable recent use of Duroc crosses on the Iberic (Extremadura Red) breed can easily destroy the special quality of 'jabugo'. Exclusivity has been taken a step further in Italy where legislation permits brand-marked Parmesan cheese and Fontina cheese to be manufactured only from the milk of the local Reggiana and Valdostana breeds of cattle respectively.

Breeders are becoming increasingly aware of the opportunity to exploit the association of rare breeds with non-intensive, welfare-friendly and environmentally-sensitive systems of production which will enhance the marketability of their products. The special quality of products from rare breeds, such as Hebridean sheep and rare breeds of pigs and poultry as detailed elsewhere, is an added bonus.

The revival of self-sufficiency systems and organic farming methods is in tune with these developments. Within such systems, the various facets of the enterprise are closely integrated. The cow relies on grass and hay to produce milk; the whey and buttermilk can be used to feed the pig, and manure from all livestock can be used on the land. In general, the minority breeds are well suited to tolerate these conditions. Working horses also fit the pattern well, deriving their energy from home-grown grass and providing manure, which is returned to the pasture. Even on some more orthodox agricultural holdings horses are coming back into favour. Dales Ponies are used on hill

*Cotswold sheep in 1866, from a painting by R. Whitford. Originally the breed was a fine-woolled type, but became a longwool breed as a result of repeated crossing with Leicester and Lincoln sheep*

farms and heavy draught breeds in lowland areas, while the breweries have discovered the value of Shire horses.

A more unusual example is provided by poultry. In trials for non-chemical pest control conducted by Rodale Institute Research Centre in Pennsylvania an old traditional poultry breed, the Dominique, proved most effective for the control of plum curculio in a 4-hectare orchard

## Horses

Pure horse breeds have suffered from the pressure of two very different effects. The development of mechanised power has had a devastating effect on heavy horse breeds, while increased leisure time and the associated demand for 'performance' riding horses has been equally damaging to middle-weight breeds.

The five years following the Second World War in the United Kindom saw the displacement of the heavy draught horse by the tractor. Up to 5000 Shire mares were being registered each year at the end of World War I, whereas the figure was a mere 200 in 1950, and the same applied to all the

*Percheron stallion, Pinchbeck Union Crest (1964-1988), owned by George Sneath of Spalding in Lincolnshire. His weight varied from 2520 lb (1143 kg) to 2632 lb (1194 kg) and he stood 17.2 hh (1.78 m), yet he has the relatively refined head resulting from the introduction of Arab or other Oriental blood into the breed*

heavy breeds. They were largely saved by the breweries, and Shire horses particularly have been in regular use with Whitbreads, Vaux and Wadworths. Time and motion studies carried out by the breweries have shown that horses are cheaper, more efficient and less of a pollution problem than motor transport for short-haul deliveries of up to five kilometres from the brewery. A machine is a depreciating asset from the moment of its purchase, but a horse not only appreciates in value, it can also produce its own replacement. On farms, the heavy horse is better suited than a tractor for tasks such as carting fodder for cattle, pulling light harrows, or even ploughing under difficult conditions. More recently, an ancient use has been revived in North America, where the demand for Shire horses as chargers in mock jousting recalls its descent from the old Black War Horse that carried armoured knights into battle.

The most important breeds of heavy horse are found in the Low Countries, France and Great Britain. The oldest is the Ardennes, which is found in France, Belgium and, more recently, in Sweden, where it is by far the most popular breed. The French Ardennes is light and hardy; it can tolerate difficult conditions of climate and feeding better than any other heavy breed. The breed's descent from upland stock makes it ideally suited for hill work. Animals of this breed have been imported by an English farmer who explains: 'My farming enterprise would not justify the cost of a huge four wheel drive tractor which would be needed on some of the hills in winter. It is safer and cheaper for a horse to cart half a dozen bales of hay across to one of the fields on this sort of hill farm. The Ardennes horses seem to thrive on poorish going, having low maintenance requirements.' A heavier type found in Belgium is the result of crossing with the Belgian Heavy Draught or Brabancon, a direct descendant of the Ardennes which has inherited the old colours of sorrel and dun. The Brabançon has massive, well-muscled shoulders and quarters, and it has been exported widely to North America for use on farms and logging camps. The Guinness Book of Records gives as the heaviest horse in the world 'Brooklyn Supreme', a Belgian stallion 19.2 hands high, who died in 1948 at twenty years of age and weighed 1455 kg.

The Shire is generally recognised as the largest heavy breed. Stallions stand just over 17 hands high on average and, in working condition, weigh about 940 kg. On a heavy clay and peat farm in Yorkshire, Shire horses carry out all the cultivations on the arable land. Compared with a tractor they are economical, and virtually break even in cost by producing their own replacements. A

*Suffolk Punch team ploughing in competition*

young horse comes into full work at almost 3½ years old and, on average, will have a 16-year working life. The Shire is not renowned for its speed of work, but it is strong, steady and reliable. The head is heavy and rather coarse, but the bone is correspondingly strong and the body short, compact and well muscled. The legs are feathered both at the back and the sides, which is attractive in the show ring but a disadvantage in the mud of arable farms. Clydesdale blood has been used to reduce the amount of feather on the legs, and the relationship between the two breeds is very close. The Clydesdale is rather more narrow and leggy than the Shire, and has feather only on the back of the legs. It is noted for its freedom from leg troubles and works at a faster pace, although it may not quite compare with the Shire for weight and strength. The average height of Clydesdale stallions is 17.2 hands and of mares 16.2 hands.

Most of the remaining breeds of heavy horse are relatively clean-legged, and the third British breed, the Suffolk Punch, resembles more closely the continental breeds. It is an elegant animal with good action both at the walk and the trot, and invariably chestnut in colour. All Suffolk Punch horses can trace their ancestry to Crisp's Horse (foaled in 1768) who stood only 15.2 hands high. The legs are short and the average height of present-day animals is only about 16 hands, but a stallion in working condition weighs about 900 kg, and the breed's pulling power is widely known. The Suffolk Punch can tolerate exposure and scarcity and are able to thrive under poor conditions. The Percheron is another heavy breed that shows remarkable stamina in the trot, and it can act in all gears. The admixture of a considerable amount of Oriental blood has resulted in much variation in type, but the breed is noted for its good, hard, blue hooves, clean legs and grey or black colour; the head is relatively small and fine, the shoulders are deep and well-laid, and the quarters wide and well-proportioned.

Two other French breeds, the Breton and Trait du Nord, have been developed to work in difficult conditions. The Trait du Nord is a strong, heavy horse, short in the leg and deep in the chest, with a docile temperament and great resistance to rough climates. The Breton has been evolved in Brittany on poor land exposed to severe winter weather; as a result it is hardy, strong and able to thrive on indifferent food.

The middleweight group of breeds includes the Cleveland Bay, Welsh Cob, and formerly the Devon Packhorse which is now extinct. These breeds have been used for farm work, but their qualities lend themselves to a wide range of uses. The Cleveland Bay stands about 16 hands high, and is bay or brown in colour with black points. The breed was developed from the native horses

*Cleveland Bay stallion, Winscombe Archibald, at 6 years of age. This breed varies in type, and currently animals which are suitable for carriage driving are preferred to the 'farming' and 'chapman' types*

of North Yorkshire and was originally used by travelling salesmen, called chapmen, before the advent of coaches. It had a long, strong back for carrying both pack and pillion, and it proved such an excellent cross with the Thoroughbred that the value of the halfbreds drastically reduced the amount of pure-breeding. It is now in demand for use in carriage driving competitions and to draw the royal coaches in London, while horses with Cleveland Bay blood have won Olympic medals for show jumping. The dominant sire-line influences are Cholderton Druid (1859) and Lord Fairfax (1875), but the genetic base is still reasonably wide. A unique blood type has been identified in the breed.

The changing use of the middleweight breeds has placed the survival of many of them at risk. Breeds such as the Hungarian Nonius, the Oldenberg, Holstein, Hanoverian and Trakehner in Germany and the Cleveland Bay and Irish Draught in the British Isles may retain their name as a token but their original type and function in many cases has been lost. The Nonius was founded in 1816 at the Mezohegyes Stud by an Anglo-Norman stallion and became a reliable and willing light draught horse of importance, both in war and agriculture; the Oldenberg was a coach horse which is now reduced to a few mares; the Trakehner has great endurance while the Hanoverian was formerly an ideal carriage horse. The increasing demand for a 'performance' sport horse is superseding other demands and all these pure breeds are in danger of being submerged in an homogenised Warmblood type.

This occurs most readily where a breed registry such as that for the Hanoverian is opened to other breeds, quickly leading to a new breed or type which is selected specifically to breed horses suitable for eventing, show-jumping, dressage, carriage driving or hunting. The most common introduction is the Thoroughbred because of its spirit, elegance and stamina. However, it often lacks bone, may be suspect in intelligence and temperament and has a flat galloping action. These deficiencies can be balanced by the strength, temperament and action of the Cleveland Bay to breed carriage horses or by the substance, courage and common sense of the Irish Draught to produce show-jumpers. However, the merging of these disparate qualities into a generalised 'gene pool' may prove a short-term solution and the future would be better served by the maintenance of the distinctive qualities of each breed in a pure-bred 'gene bank'. For some, such as the Hanoverian or the Irish Draught, it may be too late – their genome has suffered irreversible introgression of Thoroughbred genes. For others, it may still be possible to save the pure breed.

RIGHT:

*Dales Pony, Black Diamond, at 34 years of age on the author's Wiltshire farm. She was a typical working pony, bred on a Pennine hill farm by the author's father*

BELOW RIGHT:

*Dales Pony, Stainton Darkie, owned by the Fitzgerald family, competing in the driving trials at Holker Hall in the southern Lake District. The high knee action is typical of the breed*

Many of the European pony breeds have lost their true identity as a result of crossing with the Arab. In the British Isles, the New Forest, Dartmoor, Welsh and Connemara ponies have been changed in character by this means. The breeds that have remained relatively free of Oriental influence can be divided into two groups. The Friesian, Highland, Fell, Dales and the extinct Galloway belong to the larger type, capable of heavy work. The Dales Pony, in particular, was the main source of power on many Pennine hill farms until the late 1950s. In the winter of 1947, when severe storms isolated many farms for several weeks, these ponies were the only means, apart from helicopters, of getting hay to the sheep stranded on the blizzard-swept moors. The height is about 14.2 hands, and the colour most commonly black. The feet may be white, and this point distinguishes the Dales from its close relative, the whole-coloured Fell Pony. According to an old rhyme, the number of white feet is a valuable guide to quality:

*Tandem team of grey Caspians, Hopstone Mustapha (stallion) and Hopstone Chahar-Shambe (gelding), in the 1986 National Carriage Driving Championships; owned and driven by Mrs Christine Belton*

> One white foot, buy him;
> Two white feet, try him;
> Three white feet, pass by him;
> Four white feet, don't go nigh him!

During the eighteenth and nineteenth centuries the Dales Pony was used as a pack-horse to carry lead from the mines in the hills to the coast, travelling up to 400 km each week with loads of 200 kg. It needed to be strong, sure-footed and sound, and remains a hardy, long-lived breed that is remarkably free from inherited weakness such as ringbone and spavin. My own mare, Black Diamond, who had one white foot, was healthy and active, with a free, straight trot, until she died at thirty-seven years of age.

The smaller pony breeds are strong for their size. They include the Haflinger, a nimble mountain pony from Austria, chestnut in colour with a flaxen mane and tail; the Fjord, a Norwegian dun pony with a dark dorsal stripe; the Icelandic, a sturdy, docile pony whose natural riding gait is the amble; and the Exmoor, which has been used by generations of hill farmers for shepherding, and is capable of carrying a fully-grown man for a day's hunting. The genetic base of the breed has been reduced by the dominance of Caractactus (1/9), and his grandson Heatherman (78/2), in the pedigrees of present-day stock. There are now less than 150 pure breeding mares running in their original environment on Exmoor.

The Caspian is a similar size to the Exmoor, but it is a small horse rather than a pony. It was almost extinct when it was rediscovered in 1965 in northern Iran. It is a native of stony, hilly ground, and its oval, box-like, extremely tough hooves indicate its origins. It is nimble and sure-footed and does not need shoeing. Caspian horses stand 10.3 to 12.3 hands high and are characteristically narrow. As foals they have a distinctive vaulted forehead, and the muzzle is fine and tapering. The angled hocks, for which they are sometimes criticised, are simply another indication of their mountain ancestry and a factor which contributes to their startling acceleration and jumping ability.

Although horses have a long breeding life, their low reproductive rate and their relatively poor efficiency of breeding do not assist conservation programmes. Whereas a calving percentage of 94% or a lambing percentage of 100–200% are normally achieved, horses are likely to achieve less than one live foal for two mares mated, and many mares are not mated each year.

*Breeding Results for Suffolk Horses*
*1989 covering season*

| Stallions Used | Mares | | | Foals | | |
| | Covered | Not-in-foal | Aborted | Total | Live | Born dead |
| --- | --- | --- | --- | --- | --- | --- |
| 14 | 90 | 35 | 7 | 48 | 41 | 7 |

## Cattle

At various times in the past, idealists and romantics have attempted to find or create a wonder breed that will outshine all rivals. While some have enjoyed a transient success, none has been able to hold the stage for more than a few decades. In Great Britain, each century has seen a dominant breed, with the Longhorn of the eighteenth century giving way to the Shorthorn, which was itself superseded by the Friesian about sixty years ago. Similarly, the Friesian usurped the dominant position of the Normande in France. Who knows which breed will take the major role in the twenty-first century? Attention moves from breed to breed because they are all roughly equal in terms of efficiency, and success is determined mainly by fashion and consumer demand. A breed that is in danger today may shortly find itself predominant. So the fortunes of dairy cattle fluctuate in balance and opposition to those of dual-purpose breeds, and breeds with protein-rich milk may gain at the expense of those with a high fat content, but these are simply changes of emphasis not closely related to biological efficiency. It is possible to get out of an animal only what is put in, and it has been demonstrated that the Feed Conversion Rate differences between cattle breeds are negligible when animals are measured at the same rate of fatness.

Changes also take place within breeds, and comparisons which are valid today may be unrealistic in 50 or 100 years' time. When the feed requirements of various breeds of cattle were investigated at the Pan-American Exhibition in Buffalo, New York, in 1901, it was found that 146 Canadienne cows could be kept on the same amount of food as 100 Holstein cows. At that time the Canadienne closely resembled the Jersey, to which it is related, weighed only 350–380 kg, and was fawn or brown. Now it is darker, with some shading of brown, and cows weigh 500 kg. An eight-year-old cow, Bernier 2C (8070), grand Champion at L'Exposition de Quebec in 1933 and a model for the breed, was very similar to a Kerry, but Montagne Marsouin Pierrette (60641), a high-yielding cow in the 1980s, betrays evidence of Brown Swiss influence which has reduced the genetic importance of the breed.

Among minority breeds of cattle, the Dutch Belted holds pride of place because it can achieve yields of milk comparable to the Friesian–Holstein in amount, but of higher quality with fat globules that are exceptionally small. Dutch Belted cattle are jet black except for a white belt encircling the body between shoulder and hips. The cattle were originally imported to America in 1838 by the US Consul in Holland and, shortly afterwards, by the great showman Barney Barnum for exhibition in his circus. He soon discovered that they were not only beautiful animals but also excellent milkers.

In contrast, the Kerry is a small dairy animal, suited to the less fertile areas in western Ireland where it was the dominant breed little more than a century ago. At that time Kerry cattle were found in a variety of colours, but they are now black except for such small groups as the line-backed Drimmon cattle. Their graceful dairy conformation and slender upturned horns give Kerry cows an alert and attractive quality. They are hardy, adaptable and capable of subsisting on scanty

LEFT:
*Prizewinning Kerry cow. In the Livestock Breeding Act of 1925, the Irish Government defined a Kerry Cattle Area in which only Kerry bulls could be used; an early example of genetic conservation*

BELOW LEFT:
*Prizewinning Vosgienne bull, Tony, at 2½ years of age, from north-eastern France. This breed is not immediately endangered*

fare, yet several cows, with an average weight of only about 370 kg, have exceeded a lifetime production of 45,000 kg of milk. Unfortunately, very few are now recorded for milk production.

The Gloucester is a line-backed breed that has always been restricted mainly to its native county. It is a medium-sized, horned breed, and originally was a dairy animal. However, its yield was too low to compete successfully with other breeds, although the milk was used in the manufacture of Double Gloucester cheese.

A small population size and lack of demand for bulls provides no incentive for breeders to record milk yields. The resulting inability to identify superior cows as potential dams of bulls leads

RIGHT:
*Froment du Léon cow, 1972, from northern France. This is one of the most seriously endangered breeds of French cattle, with only 30 cows remaining in 9 herds in 1985*

BELOW RIGHT:
*Red Poll heifers in Berkshire before the Second World War. Although it is now a rare breed in Great Britain, the Red Poll has been exported to several other countries*

to a self-perpetuating decline. The Rare Breeds Survival Trust has recognised this problem and provides financial incentives for milk recording.

Of the sixteen breeds of French cattle that are in serious danger, nine are mainly dairy breeds, and some can produce very creditable milk records, with outstanding yields from individual cows. In particular, a cow from the line-backed Vosgienne breed yielded 40,808 kg milk in ten lactations at 4 per cent butter-fat, while a Froment du Léon cow yielded 45,716 kg milk in six lactations at 3.77 per cent butter-fat. The Froment du Léon is related closely to the Guernsey, which it resembles in colour, but its horns are lyre-shaped, and the similarity of this breed to some cattle of the

LEFT:
*The dark colour of this Gloucester cow probably indicates that she was of Bathurst descent with Friesian blood in her ancestry*

BELOW LEFT:
*Shetland cows in the Knocknagael herd, owned by the Department of Agriculture and Fisheries for Scotland, grazing moorland near Inverness*

Shetland breed in the early years of the twentieth century may be significant.

In Italy the Parmesan cheese industry was based on the protein rich milk of the currently endangered Reggiana and Modenese breeds, but all dairy breeds have declined before the invasion of the ubiquitous Holstein-Friesian.

In the British Isles, it is the dual-purpose breeds which have suffered the most severe decline in popularity, and the Shetland is included in this category. There are at present fewer than 200 breeding Shetland cows, but their hardiness, thriftiness and ease of calving deserve wider recognition. Originally the Shetland was a crofting cow in its native islands, but a herd was established near Inverness by the Department of Agriculture and Fisheries for Scotland in 1958, and during the 1970s several herds were established in England with the author's help. In 1983 a breeding group

*Kate, Norfolk Red heifer, winner of 1st prize at the Smithfield Club Show in 1867, and painted by A. M. Gauci the following year*

was sent to help to restock the Falkland Islands at the end of the hostilities. The genetic base of the Shetland was reduced in its native islands in the early 1980s by the dominance of the Knocknagael Rory line, but this problem has now been rectified as a result of incentives given to the Breed Society by the Rare Breeds Survival Trust. The whims of fashion have changed the Shetland from a predominantly dun to an exclusively black and white breed within the last sixty years, yet the neighbouring black Kyloes of the nineteenth century have meanwhile become the modern dun Highland. These cattle earned the name of Kyloe by swimming the kyles (straits) on the way from the Isle of Skye to markets on the mainland.

The Irish Moiled, the British White and the Red Poll are all polled dual-purpose breeds that claim a Scandinavian ancestry. The Irish Moiled is the rarest breed of cattle in Britain and came very close to extinction in the 1970s. It has the typical line-backed (ring-straked) colour pattern now, but one of the most famous foundation cows, Greyabbey Kate, who at 16–18 years of age averaged 8818 kg milk per lactation at 4.3 per cent butter-fat, was spotted. The ring-straked colour was adopted officially by the Breed Society after it was formed in 1926. The British White is now selected as a beef breed, but it was a dairy breed until recent years. The Red Poll was developed from the crossing of the Red Norfolk with the Suffolk Dun to combine the hardiness and beefing qualities of the former with the outstanding milking ability of the latter. The colour is red, preferably a deep shade. In 1961 imported Red Dane cattle were used in an unsuccessful attempt to raise the productivity, and this placed the breed's purity at risk. As a pure-bred the Red Poll cannot equal the milk yield of the Friesian, but its lower requirement for high-energy feed, its greater longevity, and the superior quality of its milk can make it a more profitable breed.

In the Pennine range of hills two hardier dual-purpose breeds were found. The Blue Albion, centred in the uplands of Derbyshire, flourished briefly between the two World Wars, but it is doubtful if any pure specimens can be found now. The Northern Dairy Shorthorn evolved from the pre-Colling Teeswater cattle in the undisturbed isolation of the Yorkshire Dales, with a slight influence of Ayrshire blood in the 1920s and 1930s. They were attractive animals with an alert, stylish quality and characteristic 'cocky' horns, but they have now been absorbed into the wider embrace of Coates' Herd Book.

The Dexter's ability to thrive in difficult conditions is due to its small size. Show-ring fashion

LEFT:
*Belted Galloway cattle, which have benefited from a recent demand for export to Germany where beef production in less-favoured areas is subsidised*

BELOW LEFT:
*White Park bull, Dynevor Samson, and a cow; both were still breeding at 16 years of age. From the ninth to the thirteenth centuries, Dynevor Castle was the military and political centre of South Wales, and the white cattle were an important part of its culture even at that time*

has placed much emphasis on its height at the withers (an average adult Dexter cow measures 100 cm), but selection by body weight would more accurately reflect the real value of the breed. It does not poach the land as much as heavier breeds, and its feed requirement is only 60 per cent of the Friesian's need.

The hardiest minority breeds of cattle are colour variations of the Galloway and Welsh breeds. It was fashion again that decided arbitrarily, when a Breed Society was formed in Wales in 1904, that the breed should be called the Welsh Black, with all other colours excluded. For the whole of this century the Belted Welsh (Bolian Gwynion), White Welsh, the reds, duns, yellows, smokies and blues, have been outcasts of the pedigree world. Now, at last, they have been gathered together under an organisation named Gwartheg Hynafol Cymru (Ancient Cattle of Wales). The Galloway situation is very similar. Black was the chosen colour, although dun animals were accepted. Other

*Longhorn bull, Watling Samson, when he was the stock bull at Winthill Farm*

colours were excluded, and the Belted Galloway formed its own Society in 1921, later extended to include a section for the White Galloway. These breeds can winter on rough hill grazing and have, under their long outer coat of hair, a dense, mossy undercoat for protection from harsh weather. The belted colour pattern is derived from the Lakenvelder cattle of Holland. The breed's name is a combination of laken (sheet) and veld (field), and the idea persists in the names of the Belted cattle and the extinct Sheeted Somerset. The colour pattern of the White Galloway and the White Welsh is the same as that of the White Park.

The White Park does not fit neatly into any category. Historically, its course has been unusual, taking it from the sacrificial altars of the Druids to the hunting chases of the Plantagenet monarchs and the country parks of stately homes. At Dynevor in Wales in the nineteenth century White Park bullocks were used as draught animals, and more recently White Park cows were milked in both the Dynevor and Faygate herds. Indeed, Faygate Garter yielded 5469 kg milk at 5.04 per cent butter-fat in her second lactation. However, it is as a beef breed that the White Park is now starting to play a valuable role. The cows are large (630–650 kg) and easy-calving. With the swing away from fat-beef carcasses, the bulls are finding increasing favour as sires of easily born, fast-growing calves with a high yield of lean meat. In studies of genetic distancing, it has been shown that the White Park is not closely related to other British breeds, and thus its crossbred progeny exhibit considerable hybrid vigour. The head of a White Park bull was a most auspicious choice as the symbol of the Rare Breeds Survival Trust, for no other breed expresses to the same extent the merging of historical significance with commercial potential, and of sentiment with the objective merit of genetic uniqueness, that represents the contrasting values of the old native breeds. The White Park dominated the cattle section for the first decade of the Rare Breeds Survival Trust's Show and Sale, winning the Interbreed Championship on seven occasions, and cattle of this breed have now been exported to Canada, USA, Australia, France, Denmark and Germany.

The Longhorn is similar in type and purpose to the White Park. Originally it was a triple purpose breed, yielding milk of a high quality – it was claimed that more butter could be made from Longhorn milk than from the same quantity of milk produced by any other breed. It was improved first in the Craven district of Yorkshire, before being modified and popularised in the Midlands of England. It is not related to the Texas Longhorn, but resembles it in having horns of a distinctive and eye-catching character. They sweep backwards from the convex forehead in a variety of styles, and are fine in texture and free from any black coloration. The Longhorn's coat varies in colour from dark plum-brindle to light roan, but a white stripe down the back and tail and white patches on each thigh are characteristic of the breed. It re-emerged into the commercial world after it won the Burke Trophy for the best pair of beef animals at the Royal Show in 1981, but this commercial emphasis has dangerous side-effects. The genetic base of the breed was reduced dangerously by the imposition of a minimum-weight standard for bulls of 400 kg at 400 days of age, and an analysis carried out by the author in 1987 showed that three bulls had contributed 49.47 per cent of the ancestry of the breed. It is possible that one of these bulls has Shorthorn and/or Aberdeen Angus blood in his pedigree.

The Beef Shorthorn is a specialist beef breed that was bred for extreme early maturity and blocky conformation, and lost both growth rate and leanness in the process. In 1974 the average 400-day weight of bulls was only 411 kg. It lost popularity with the changing market demand in the second half of the twentieth century, and in 1985 only 185 heifers and 94 bulls were registered. An attempt was made to remedy the situation by crossing with the related Maine–Anjou, but in 1987 the breed was recognised as a rare breed by the Rare Breeds Survival Trust, with the aim of keeping it free from outside influences.

## Sheep

Sheep breeds can be divided conveniently into distinct categories. At one extreme there are the breeds which are described, sometimes incorrectly, as primitive and can be found mainly around the north-western seaboard of Europe. They often follow a pattern of low metabolic activity in the autumn and winter which makes it very difficult to put on flesh during this period. Next are the hill and mountain breeds, noted for their hardiness and frequenting the most difficult terrain. The longwool breeds are found in kinder conditions and are kept for one of two purposes: some for the production of heavyweight lambs and wool, and some to sire prolific daughters. The shortwool breeds are used either to sire the finished lambs as the end product of breeding programmes, or in self-contained pure-breeding flocks. Finally, there are special breeds which do not fit clearly into any category.

The most primitive breed is the Soay, which has survived on the exposed islands of St Kilda beyond the Outer Hebrides. The short-stapled fleece, a mixture of hair and wool, is shed naturally and may be used for hand-spinning, although it is more difficult to handle than other wools. Soay rams are sometimes used on ewe hoggs of other breeds to ensure easy lambing, but more usually Soay ewes are mated to rams of meat breeds, such as Ryeland or Dorset Down, when the crossbred lambs will be as heavy as their dams by about twelve weeks of age. The Soay does not suffer from footrot or fly strike under normal farming conditions. In the future, it is possible that the quality of the Soay carcass will be a major factor in its success. As a pure-bred it is a very efficient producer of lean meat which has the added attraction of a distinctive flavour.

The natural qualities of the Soay have been preserved in the feral flock of 1500 sheep on the island of Hirta. The semi-feral flocks of North Ronaldsay sheep on their native island and on the

ABOVE:
*A Mouton d'Ouessant ram at 2 years of age*

ABOVE RIGHT:
*A Manx Loghtan ram with an imposing head; he is shedding his fleece*

island of Linga Holm, off the west coast of the island of Stronsay, will serve a similar purpose. The North Ronaldsay sheep is particularly important because of its ability to exist on a diet of seaweed. Mature ewes weigh about 25 kg and, like the Soay, are primitive and fine-boned with a short tail. All the rams, and about 20 per cent of the ewes, are horned. The rams grow a fringe of coarse, dark hair which runs down the underside of the neck to the chest, in contrast to Soay rams which develop a hairy mane on top of the neck and shoulders.

It is likely that similar sheep were found previously in other outposts of the British Isles. The Cladagh (literal meaning is 'shore sheep'), which is only recently extinct and last survived on the Aran Islands off the west coast of Ireland, was a primitive, short-tailed, seaweed-eating breed with coloured wool, very similar to the North Ronaldsay.

Shetland sheep also possess a short, flat fluke-shaped tail, but they cannot be described realistically as a primitive breed. Their wool is softer and finer than that of any other British breed and occurs in a variety of natural colours. Mature ewes weigh about 37 kg and are polled, while the rams carry small, smooth horns. There was some crossing with introduced breeds during the nineteenth century and a Breed Society was formed in 1927 to combat this trend. The Castlemilk Moorit was created as a separate breed in Scotland early in the twentieth century, and the Shetland may have been used in the programme. However, the main influences were Soay and Manx Loghtan. The Castlemilk Moorit carries the moufflon colour pattern and both sexes are horned. The breed was recognised by the Rare Breeds Survival Trust in 1983.

The Manx Loghtan is often included in the primitive category, but it differs in several respects. It is multihorned, larger in size with mature ewes weighing about 40 kg on lowland pasture, and the tail is longer, reaching almost to the hocks and described as 'half-length'. The fleece of the

ABOVE LEFT:
*A Castlemilk Moorit ewe with twin lambs*

ABOVE:
*A Whitefaced Woodland ewe and lamb.*
*A related breed, the Silverdale or Limestone,*
*was found in the Kendal/Carnforth area,*
*and the last flock died out at Hutton Roof*
*in 1915*

Manx Loghtan is moorit, although other colours were present a hundred years ago, and the moorit colour was fixed by John Caesar Bacon who saved the breed at the end of the nineteenth century and introduced a little Shetland blood. Some present day animals carry the moufflon pattern from the use of a Soay ram on the Isle of Man in 1956. The true colour is best seen in young lambs before the wool fades from exposure to bleaching agents such as sunlight. It can be woven into very attractive, natural-coloured worsted material, but the wool quality does vary and some fleeces contain a considerable amount of kemp. Manx Loghtans are claimed to be free from fly strike, and to be long-lived. A 15-year-old ewe in the Riber Castle flock had a full set of teeth when inspected by the author in 1977. Breeders of Manx Loghtan sheep on the mainland of Britain currently place much emphasis on wool yield, while breeders on the Isle of Man focus more on the desirability of the multi-horned characteristic and close, short- stapled wool. In practice, there is considerable variation in type at both locations. Fleece type varies from dense, fine wool to a more open coarse staple; the mean fibre diameter varies from 27 to 37 microns; and the variation in the density of pigmentation allows considerable opportunity for the selection which inevitably follows characterisation surveys.

The Hebridean is a closely-related but slightly smaller animal (mature ewe weight of 36 kg), which produces black or dark-brown wool that is much sought after for hand-spinning. The black wool has a longer staple, a higher lustre, and grows silvery with age as grey fibres appear in the fleece. Hebrideans are also noted for their longevity, and a Leckford ewe in the Ash flock was still producing triplets in her late teens. Claims that primitive unselected breeds produce higher quality and healthier meat have been given support by recent studies. Lipid analysis research has shown that Hebridean sheep have a lower level of cholesterol and undesirable saturated fats (palmitic, stearic etc.), and a much higher level of desirable polyunsaturated fats, especially the C18 long chain fatty acids (linolenic, linoleic, etc.) than popular commercial breeds.

Primitive breeds in other European countries have not retained the same degree of purity as their British counterparts. The Ushant sheep, which formerly inhabited the island of Ouessant off the western tip of Finistère, bears some resemblance to a two-horned Hebridean. They were very small, meaty, black sheep, that were recorded as early as the seventeenth century, but between 1904 and 1910 white sheep from the Arrée mountains on the mainland were introduced and mated with the native breed, so that now 75 per cent of the sheep are white. Similarly, the Dutch Heath sheep, which are preserved in Holland, are a mixture of two native, primitive types, the Drenthe and the Veluwe. A third type, the Kemper, is extinct. The German Heath or Heidschnucke (heather sheep) combines the primitive feature of a short tail with a coarse fleece and a dark face, and is reminiscent of the feral Boreray in Britain.

*The head of a Norfolk Horn ram c 1800. (From a painting signed Weaver 1807). After 1919 this breed survived only in the flock of James Sayer at Bury St Edmunds*

The basis of the British sheep industry, and the first step in the system of stratification which provides the foundation of crossbreeding, are the mountain breeds that roam the highlands of Scotland, the mountains of Wales and the Pennines. In the midst of the black-faced breeds from the southern parts of the Pennines can be found a sheep that differs from the standard pattern in having a white face with a pink or partly pink nose; it has finer, softer wool and it is larger. The Whitefaced Woodland took its name from a valley, Woodland Dale, in northern Derbyshire, but it is also known as the Penistone, after the nearby market town in Yorkshire where a sheep fair has been held since 1699. In 1971 show classes for the breed were started again after a lapse of twenty years. The breed arose from the same foundation stocks as its black-faced neighbours, the Swaledale and Lonk, but crosses with the Cheviot and, later, the Merino changed its type. Mature ewes on lowland pasture weigh about 60 kg, and the rams are used for crossing to increase the size of other hill breeds.

Another breed which does not fit neatly into a standard category of breeds is the Norfolk Horn. Originally one of the black-faced hill breeds, the Norfolk Horn evolved in the relative isolation of East Anglia and was adapted to exploit the poor, acid heathland in that area. It developed a close fleece to withstand the bitter east winds blowing unhindered from central Europe, but dispensed with the long outer coat which the Pennine breeds needed to shed the rain in wetter areas. The last pure Norfolk Horn animal died in 1973, but a breeding-back programme had already been established, using the Suffolk breed which was itself created by crossing the Norfolk Horn with the Southdown. This programme successfully fixed the characteristics of the old breed, and the Norfolk Horn was recognised again by the Rare Breeds Survival Trust in 1986. It is horned in both sexes, long-legged and active.

Wales seems to have assumed the responsibility for conserving the colour varieties of popular breeds, as we have seen already with cattle. Among the Welsh Mountain sheep, the Black Welsh Mountain has its own Breed Society, and the Balwen, Torwen and Torddu have followed suit more recently. The Torddu, or Badger-faced, bears some resemblance to the primitive, extinct Rhiw sheep, but in all except colour it is a Welsh Mountain. Both names are descriptive: dark stripes down the face suggest badger markings, while a dark line down the neck leads to a 'black belly', the literal translation of Torddu.

In France the system of stratification is not practised within the sheep industry, so that the minority hill breeds differ widely in type and function. The Thones et Marthod and the Brigasque are both hardy milking breeds found on the Italian border; the Lourdaise is a primitive type of Merino from the Spanish border; while the Rouge du Roussillon, or Barbarine, found on the Mediterranean coast, is probably descended from North African sheep. The Bizet, a leggy animal from the Massif Central, with coarse wool and spiralled horns in the male, comes nearest to the British hill sheep type but, like many continental breeds, the Bizet is able to give birth at intervals of eight months, whereas British hill breeds have a limited breeding season.

In Britain hill ewes are moved from the uplands to gentler terrain after they have produced three crops of lambs. There they are mated to crossing rams in order to produce daughters which will themselves be used as breeding animals. The rams belong to high-performance breeds, including those longwool breeds which suffered least from Bakewell's attentions and retained their prolificacy and milking ability.

*Comparative Performance of Minority, Native and Imported Crossing Breeds of Sheep*
(from data published by ARFC / ITOVIC / LIS / MLC)

| Breed | Category | Lambing % (live lambs) | Lamb growth (50-day wt)* | Productivity Index |
|---|---|---|---|---|
| DUAL-PURPOSE (CROSSING AND MEAT) | | | | |
| British Milksheep | Native | 252 | 107.8 | 163.0 |
| Wensleydale | Minority | 168 | 103.0 | 137.6 |
| Rouge de l'Ouest | Imported | 174 | 96.3 | 132.9 |
| Bleu du Maine | Imported | 174 | 92.1 | 129.0 |
| CROSSING: | | | | |
| Bluefaced Leicester | Native | 199 | 100.2 | 142.8 |
| Teeswater | Minority | 186 | 102.4 | 141.5 |
| Colbred | Native | 182 | 102.0 | 140.2 |
| Cambridge | Native | 238 | 86.3 | 139.6 |
| Border Leicester | Native | 162 | 100.0 | 133.3 |
| Oldenberg | Imported | 161 | 93.0 | 126.6 |

*Lamb growth rate is expressed as an index, taking the Border Leicester as 100.

Two of these, the Wensleydale and the Teeswater, are now minority breeds. The Teeswater, one of the largest and most ancient longwool breeds, was noted at an early stage for its prolificacy, with

ABOVE:
*A British Milksheep ewe, Gallowshieldrigg Stalie 14th, with triplet lambs by Pollux*

ABOVE RIGHT:
*Teeswater; an old longwool breed*

even quadruplets and quintuplets recorded. In 1802 a group of twenty-four ewes produced seventy lambs, and the main purpose of the Teeswater is to sire Masham ewes, which is a prolific crossbred sheep.

The Wensleydale is also used to sire Mashams, and it is closely related to the Teeswater. The foundation ram of the breed was 'Blue Cap', born in 1839 from a Teeswater ewe by a Leicester ram. He 'possessed a wonderfully broad masculine head of a deep blue colour', and this pigmentation is now characteristic of the breed. When it was superseded by the Teeswater as a sire of prolific ewes, the Wensleydale attracted attention with its other qualities, in particular the unique characteristics of its wool. Most breeds of sheep possess certain skin follicles which produce kemp fibres, in addition to those that produce wool; but in the Wensleydale the kemp and coarse fibres are replaced by fine-wool fibres, a feature known as Central Checking. When Wensleydale rams are mated with the wool-less Wiltshire Horn, or even with hairy African sheep, the crossbred progeny grow fleeces which are free from kemp, an improvement beyond the powers of even the fine-woolled Merino. The long, lustrous, purled wool of the Wensleydale is valued for use in hand tapestry work. The Wensleydale also sires crossbred lambs with a high weight of lean meat in the carcass, but they lack the necessary conformation to exploit this quality fully. In other respects the Wensleydale is a compromise between the prolific longwools, such as the Teeswater, and those descended more directly from the Dishley Leicester.

The Lincoln, Leicester, Greyface Dartmoor and Cotswold, all large polled sheep with a whitish face, fall into the longwool category. Adult ewes weigh about 80 kg and yield a fleece of about 5½ –6 kg of curly lustrous wool. The Lincoln is rather larger and has a heavier fleece (7–8 kg) than the other breeds, but shares with them the main purpose of producing heavy lambs that are ready for slaughter at high weights at about 10 months of age. The Lincoln is the oldest longwool breed and originated on the heavy soil of its native county, where it developed into a big, slow-maturing animal. It was used by Bakewell to produce the Dishley Leicester, which was then used to improve its parent breed.

The modern Leicester is a direct descendant of the Dishley breed and is now found mainly on the Yorkshire Wolds. The line of descent from the Dishley breed is via the Colling brothers on Teesside, Sir Tatton Sykes at Sledmere, and H. P. Robinson of Carnaby near Hull. It yields a fleece of about 6 kg and has been used for the production of heavyweight hoggets, but recent work has demonstrated its potential use as the dam of a half-bred ewe. In a comparative trial, pure-bred

Leicester ewes lambed at 160 per cent, but Leicester half-bred ewes, sired by British Milksheep rams, lambed at 218 per cent with an increased yield of milk and no reduction in the value of the fleece. Since 1968 the genetic base of the breed has been very narrow; at that time only twenty-two flocks existed and the influence of one ram, Bartindale Prince Goofy, was dominant. In 1986 coloured Leicester sheep were admitted to an appendix in the Flock Book, and it seems that they may produce a superior carcass of lean meat. The Dartmoor evolved through crossing the Leicester on the native sheep of Devon; it dropped in numbers during the 1970s and 1980s and was recognised as a rare breed in 1987. In Gloucestershire, the native sheep were fine wooled as late as the early eighteenth century, but continual crosses with Leicester and Lincoln rams have created the present-day Cotswold as a typical member of the longwool group, with a fleece weight of about 5½ kg. The name is derived from the Saxon words 'cote' (sheepfold) and 'wold' (bare hill). The

OPPOSITE TOP LEFT:
*Leicester Longwool. This breed also has a coloured variety, which is a type of grey rather than black and is controlled by genes at the 'A' locus. In adult coloured sheep there is dark wool from the withers around the shoulders like a shawl*

TOP RIGHT:
*Lincoln; an old longwool breed. It was crossed with the Merino to produce the Corriedale*

BELOW LEFT:
*In the eighteenth century, the Ryeland was a fine-woolled sheep with a light fleece. Crosses with Longwool and Down breeds changed it into a meat breed*

BELOW RIGHT:
*Oxford Down*

breed was at the height of its fame in the mid-nineteenth century when as many as 5000 rams were sold or hired in a season, but by 1950 only one breeder remained, Mr W. Garne of Aldsworth.

In the neighbouring county of Hereford the most ancient shortwool breed is found. Known first as the Hereford, it was renowned for the quality of its wool 'from where you may draw a thread as fine as silk', and which was dubbed 'Lemster ore'. In the late eighteenth century the name of Ryeland was first used, and the breed was changed by crossing with Southdown and other rams, so that it now belongs to the Down group of breeds and is used to sire high-quality, lightweight lambs.

The Southdown occupies a place among shortwool breeds comparable to that of the Dishley Leicester among longwool breeds. John Ellman was the father of the Southdown. He was born at Hartfield in Sussex in 1753 and died in 1832. He succeeded to the tenancy of the 580-acre Glynde Farm near Lewes in 1780, and it was here that he took as his raw material the local heath breed of the Downs and transformed it into the blocky, compact animal now known as the Southdown. He was succeeded as doyen of the breed by Jonas Webb (1796–1862), who farmed near Cambridge and who started with Ellman stock in 1822. The sheep that these two men created and developed made a powerful impact on sheep breeding throughout Great Britain and in other parts of the world. It influenced the development of all the other Down breeds in Great Britain; exports started c.1800; the first New Zealand flock was founded in 1863, and the breed reached its zenith early in the twentieth century. British breeders have selected for shorter legs and a lighter-coloured face, and the French and New Zealand sheep probably are more representative of the original type.

At the other end of the scale from the Ryeland and Southdown, smallest of the Down breeds, is the massive Oxford Down, almost twice as heavy as the Southdown, with mature ewes weighing 90–95 kg or more. In 1920 there were almost 200 flocks and more than 27,000 ewes. By 1970 this had fallen to less than 1000 ewes in 30 flocks. Its great size is associated with a rapid growth rate and with the production of heavyweight lambs, for which purpose it is the outstanding breed. In a trial carried out by the Animal Breeding Research Organisation in Edinburgh, crossbred lambs sired by the Oxford Down grew 4 per cent faster than lambs sired by the Suffolk, 11½ per cent faster than lambs sired by the Texel, Dorset Down and Ile de France, and 16 per cent faster than those sired by the Oldenberg. There is no need to speculate in the importation of exotic breeds for the production of heavyweight lambs when we already have the Oxford Down. It was developed by crossing the Cotswold with the early Hampshire Down which was itself still in the formative stage.

*Value of Various British Breeds of Sheep for the Production of Heavyweight Lambs*

| Sire Breed | Av. birth weight kg | Av. Weaning weight kg | Av. carcass weight kg | % lambs over 22.5 kg dcw | % lambs not sold by mid-Feb. |
|---|---|---|---|---|---|
| Oxford Down | 5.3 | 28.6 | 24.9 | 64 | 8 |
| Hampshire Down | 5.0 | 26.9 | 23.1 | 27 | 9 |
| Suffolk | 4.9 | 26.5 | 22.7 | 30 | 14 |
| Lincoln | 5.9 | 26.0 | 21.8 | 23 | 28 |
| Wiltshire Horn | 5.0 | 24.9 | 21.3 | 20 | 43 |
| Cotswold | 5.3 | 24.4 | 21.3 | 7 | 25 |

In the West Midlands of England and the Welsh Borders, another member of the Down group developed from several local types. The Shropshire was derived mainly from the fine-woolled, horned Morfe Common sheep, and from those on the Longmynd and Cannock Chase, with a later, inevitable introduction of Southdown blood. The Shropshire was at the peak of its popularity around 1906, in which year more than 2000 registered animals were exported. Its reliance on export was the cause of the breed's sudden decline, because the abrupt closure of the North American market in the late 1920s left Shropshire breeders with a sheep developed for a special trade and unwanted by British flockmasters, who objected to its heavily woolled head. The modern Shropshire has a cleaner black face, with a covering of wool on the poll. It is now being selected as a typical 'meat sire' breed and is recovering popularity after falling very low in numbers.

The Rare Breeds Survival Trust has carried out commercial evaluation trials to demonstrate the potential value of the Shropshire. It performed creditably in comparison with the Suffolk. The dominance of the Suffolk, together with the popularity of some imported breeds such as the Texel and Charollais, has adversely affected most other Down breeds in the British Isles, so that breeds such as the Dorset Down need to be monitored carefully.

*Sheep Breeds, Commercial Evaluation Trials*
*Shropshire and Suffolk (1989)*

| Breed | Birth wt. | Slaughter | | | | |
|---|---|---|---|---|---|---|
| | | Age | Wt | Carcass Wt | Grade | |
| | | days | kg | kg | %1–2 | %E\U |
| **FARM 1 (JANUARY LAMBING)** | | | | | | |
| Shropshire | 4.26 | 134.3 | 36.13 | 15.42 | 80 | nil |
| Suffolk | 4.31 | 125.7 | 36.26 | 16.49 | 90 | 10.0 |
| **FARM 2 (MARCH LAMBING)** | | | | | | |
| Shropshire | 4.67 | 205 | 36.25 | 16.40 | 92 | 11.0 |
| Suffolk | 4.75 | 214 | 35.94 | 16.41 | 98 | 23.2 |

The Portland is also a shortwool breed, but of an earlier type and more closely related to the Welsh Mountain. It is a small sheep, with mature ewes weighing only 38–40 kg, and both sexes are horned. The wool is foxy-red when the lambs are born, and the face and legs are brown or tan. The wool becomes white during the first few weeks of life, but red kemp fibres can be found in the britch wool, as in the case of the Welsh Mountain. The Portland is notorious for its low prolificacy but famous for the excellent flavour of its fine-grained meat. In the mid-nineteenth century D. Low reported that 'their mutton is exceedingly delicate.' George III chose Portland mutton when he visited Dorset, and this was the theme of the first of the official dinners held by breeders of Portland sheep at the Gloucester Hotel in Weymouth in 1980. One of the popular, publicity-seeking claims about the origin of several British breeds of livestock is that they swam ashore from

*Wiltshire Horn sheep shedding 'fleece', the breed was replaced in its native county by the Southdown during the eighteenth century*

the wrecked Spanish Armada, and this glamorous myth has been extended to the Portland. It is in fact one of the old tan-faced breeds that were the original inhabitants of the British Isles. Crossed with Merino-type sheep, it gave rise to the modern Dorset Horn breed, but at the same time was probably itself influenced by the Merino, which added an extra spiral to the horns of the rams and would account for the ability of a few Portland ewes to lamb outside the normal breeding season.

In France the Solognote, also a rare breed that has attracted considerable publicity and official support in its attempts to survive, has much in common with the Portland. It is a shortwool lowland breed, yielding a fleece of about 1.35 kg of red wool. Mature ewes weigh about 55 kg and produce on average 1.4 lambs which grow at the rate of about 245 g per day. The young lambs are not easy to rear, but they are noted for the quality of their meat and as adults are thrifty and long-lived.

The Wiltshire Horn is an unusual sheep. It originally inhabited the chalkland Downs of Salisbury Plain but had been ousted by the Southdown by the end of the eighteenth century, surviving only in the Vale of the White Horse. It was forced to find refuge in the Midland counties of England and on the island of Anglesey in North Wales, which are now the main centres of the breed. It is unique among improved British breeds of sheep because it does not grow wool. Formerly it came from the white-faced, horned group of breeds in south-west England that includes the Dorset Horn and Exmoor Horn, but even by the late eighteenth century its growth of wool was sparse and often the underparts were bare. This characteristic was exaggerated by deliberate selection, so that today the Wiltshire Horn grows a thick, matted, hairy coat which peels off as the animal fattens in the early summer. The breed reached very low numbers during the early nineteenth century, and survived only by crossing with Leicester and Cotswold sheep, although the extent of the crossing has not been recorded.

## Goats

The majority of popular milking goats are derived from Swiss breeds, namely the Toggenberg, Saanen (Gessenay) and Alpine. The main exception is the Nubian which comes from Africa. It is possible that the minority breeds also found their origin in Switzerland. Certainly the similarity of Bagot goats to the Schwarzhal breed from the Canton of Valais is still strong, although they have spent 700 years in independent existence since Crusaders introduced animals of the Swiss breed to

LEFT:
*A group of Bagot goats in Cumbria at Appleby Castle, a Rare Breeds Survival Trust Approved Centre*

BELOW LEFT:
*Schwarzhal goat in Switzerland. It originated in the canton of Valais, and is known also as the Walliser and the Valaisanne à col noir*

Britain. The goats have run for most of that time as a semi-feral group in the grounds surrounding Blithfield Hall in Staffordshire, the ancestral home of the Bagot family. They have become closely associated with the family; a goat's head appeared in 1380 on the heraldic crest of Sir John Bagot and, later, on family tombstones and armour; the entrance to the park is known as Goat Lodge, and goat heads are carved in the stonework around the entire building. In the 1950s some Bagot goats were released in the Rhinog hills in Gwynedd, and the feral goats in that area still retain the Bagot colour pattern. In July 1979 the herd at Blithfield was donated to the Rare Breeds Survival Trust by Nancy Lady Bagot.

*Golden Guernsey goats vary in colour and this billy is quite pale. He sports an impressive pair of dorcas (spreading) horns*

The colouring of Bagot goats varies, but generally the head and neck are black or dark brown and the remainder of the body is white. The parent stock in Switzerland and the Rhone valley is more uniformly marked. The head, neck, shoulders and forelegs of the Schwarzhal goats are black, hence its name, and no markings appear on the rest of the body, which is white. This beautiful breed is now making a remarkable recovery after having become nearly extinct. The Bagot colour pattern was further diluted by a grading-up programme, but this was closed in 1985 when the number of grade animals exceeded the number of pure-breds. Selection for proper colour is now practised.

The Golden Guernsey goat also narrowly escaped extinction, being saved by the determination of an island breeder, Miss Milbourne, who owned the L'Ancresse herd. The origin of the Golden Guernsey is not clear: it may have been derived from Saanen stock (the Swiss name Gessenay might have been confused with Guernsey), or it may owe more of its ancestry to Syrian goats. Malta seems to have been an important staging post, and the skin of Maltese goats is a distinctive orange-red that is also seen in the Golden Guernsey. The official description of their colour is honey-gold, which might suggest a mixture of Saanen and Syrian stock – Herodotus described the Syrian goats, whose 'wondrous ears turn upwards and outwards at the tips in tribute to Apollo who gave them their golden coats'. The Golden Guernsey is a milking goat, but it is more robust than the popular breeds. The genetic base of the breed is very narrow and when I analysed the structure of the breed in 1980 I reported:

> Most lines go back to Tshombie of L'Ancresse and most of the remainder trace to Kingcup of L'Ancresse. The close relationships are intensified because Bracken, who is the dam of Tshombie's most important grandson (Marmaduke), is the full sister to Majic, who is the dam of Kingcup and of his only important son, Chestnut. Within the Tshombie line the relationships are intensified even further by the presence of influential full sibs. For example, Archibald, Alexander, Ajax and Aurelia are all by Marmaduke out of Rose, while Puck, Rapha and Rachel are all by Rufus out of Louise, and Sarnia is out of Louise by Sunny Jim, the sire of Rufus. The result of this is that all the current males are very closely related.

*Middle White sow, Wilmington Queen 4th, Breed Champion at the National Pig Breeders' Association Show at York in 1950*

## Pigs

Most British breeds of pig are of relatively recent origin. They result from the crossbreeding of native pigs with the Chinese and Neapolitan animals introduced during the late eighteenth and early nineteenth centuries. The Chinese pigs were small, fat, early maturing, and black or white in colour. Modern Chinese pigs retain these characteristics. The Meishan, which is the largest of the seven varieties of the Taihu type, weighs only 190-195 kg as an adult boar and 170-175 kg as an adult sow, while the backfat of even a ¼-bred Meishan is ten per cent thicker than that of a white European bacon pig. However, the Chinese pigs reach puberty at a remarkably early age, and have a high ovulation rate which is improved even more by hybrid vigour in crosses with European breeds.

*Hybrid Vigour produced by crossing Chinese and European pigs*

| Breed/cross | Age at puberty days | Litter size born | alive | weaned |
|---|---|---|---|---|
| Meishan | 81 | 14.9 | 14.0 | 13.1 |
| Large White/Meishan | | 15.3 | 14.5 | 12.8 |
| Large White | c.200 | 10.7 | 10.2 | 9.2 |

In contrast the large, rangy native pigs were lop-eared and came in dirty shades of ochre. These characteristics were recombined in new breeds in a variety of permutations depending on the contribution of each parental type in Great Britain. The rare breeds of pig have become so because they were not specialist 'bacon' breeds, and have not been selected intensively for growth rate and the maximum production of lean meat, as have breeds such as the Large White, Landrace, Hampshire and Duroc. However, they have retained a superior quality of meat and superior maternal qualities. Their hardiness, fecundity, milk yield and temperament are valuable attributes.

The Middle White evolved from a wider Yorkshire type that included also the Large White and the Small White. It is an extreme pork breed, white in colour with prick ears. It had fallen to very

*Wessex Saddleback sow, Merrywood Violet 16th, prize winner at the Ayr Show, 1958. The British Saddleback breed was formed by merging the Essex and Wessex breeds in 1967*

low numbers by the Second World War, but previously it enjoyed a strong export market in the Far East, especially in Japan. Its fortunes are now being revived to some degree by a demand for traditional speciality meats, and exports to Japan resumed in 1987 with a group of sixteen pigs. The Japanese held the breed in such high regard that they erected a memorial to three boars, Pendley Drummer Boy 4, Pendley Bugle Boy and Newton Firethorn.

*Comparative Performance of Some Pig Breeds taken from the*
*Cumulative Results for Four Years (1972–75 inclusive)*

| Breed | Number of litters | Pigs born per litter | Pigs reared per litter | Mortality % |
|---|---|---|---|---|
| MINORITY | | | | |
| *Pork:* | | | | |
|   Berkshire | 162 | 9.60 | 8.24 | 14.17 |
|   Middle White | 208 | 10.12 | 8.48 | 16.21 |
| | | (9.86) | (8.36) | (15.19) |
| | | | | |
| *Dual-purpose:* | | | | |
|   British Saddleback | 2571 | 10.53 | 9.2 | 12.63 |
|   Gloucester Old Spots | 497 | 10.17 | 9.02 | 11.31 |
|   Large Black | 323 | 10.49 | 9.18 | |
| | | (10.40) | (9.13) | (12.01) |
| | | | | |
| *Bacon:* | | | | |
|   Tamworth | 149 | 9.13 | 8.16 | 10.62 |
| POPULAR | | | | |
|   Large White | 66,320 | 10.38 | 8.91 | 14.16 |
| IMPORTED | | | | |
|   Hampshire | 1632 | 9.20 | 8.07 | 12.28 |

The Berkshire was developed by crossing with Chinese and Neapolitan pigs, which gave the prick ears and dished face, and changed the old rangy, black and tan Berkshire into a compact black animal. It is an early maturing, firm-fleshed pork breed, which declined with the market demand for bacon breeds. In 1976 the Rare Breeds Survival Trust imported an Australian boar, Lynjoleen Ambassador 1183rd, and he has had a beneficial influence on the breed. His progeny produced grade A carcasses without exception, and his daughter, Rumbolds Royal Lustre 7th, was not only the Interbreed Champion at the 1978 Show, but also reared thirty-seven pigs in her first three litters, with an average three-week litter weight of 74. 1 kg.

The British Saddleback resulted from the merger of the Essex and Wessex varieties in 1967. The Essex was influenced by Neapolitan imports, but the Wessex was basically a native pig and was the foundation of the Hampshire pig in North America in the early nineteenth century. The British Saddleback has been used by major breeding companies as one parent of commercial hybrids. It was selected as a parent breed of the Camborough, which was first marketed in 1979, because it was an excellent grazer with a quiet temperament, good maternal characteristics, and a degree of fatness that buffered the sow's metabolism in harsh outdoor conditions. A decision by the breeding company in 1991 to replace the British Saddleback by the Duroc was quickly regretted.

The Gloucester Old Spots is another dual-purpose breed with lop ears. Formerly known as the Orchard Pig, it evolved in the Berkeley Vale in Gloucestershire and was adapted to utilise by-products such as windfall apples and whey. More recently, a narrow hierarchical structure in the breed was based on the Ribbesford herd in Worcestershire, where the pigs were kept indoors and selected on the basis of national performance test results. This situation could have changed the character of the breed if it had persisted. Gloucester Old Spots pigs made a major contribution to the Minnesota #3 breed developed by Winters in the USA, and in 1979 a breeding group were exported to France.

The Large Black, like the British Saddleback, resulted from the amalgamation of two strains, one from East Anglia and one from South-West England. It is large and lop-eared, and it owes much of its ancestry to black Chinese and French imports. At the end of the nineteenth century it was one of the most popular breeds in Britain, but it is now numerically low. This may have resulted in part from its black skin, which gives the bacon a 'seedy cut', but it is a very good maternal breed, hardy, docile, and suitable for outdoor systems.

The Tamworth was influenced very little by Asiatic imports, and has always been a relatively

ABOVE LEFT:
*Gloucester Old Spots sow with litter*

ABOVE:
*Large Black sow with litter*

RIGHT:
*The seriously endangered Basque breed of pig from the Pyrenees has been given a new lease of life by Pierre Oteiza, whose company Vallee des Aldudes has developed speciality meat products utilising the particular qualities and characteristics of the breed*

BELOW RIGHT:
*British Lop sow. Although the British Lop is a seriously endangered breed it regularly wins Interbreed Championships in competition with popular breeds at major agricultural shows*

lean breed. Tamworth pigs were exported to North America and Australasia, and it was from Tasmania that the Rare Breeds Survival Trust imported three boars in 1976 to boost the declining bloodlines of the breed in Britain. A group of thirty Tamworths were exported to Spain in 1978 as it was considered that their hardy, thrifty characteristics suited them for crossing with the native Iberian pigs. The breed's main fault is its low fecundity.

The British Lop is the rare breed which most closely resembles the popular white breeds, and it may have been influenced to some degree by Landrace introductions. It was previously known as the National Long White Lop-Eared, but it has remained for the most part a local breed in Cornwall. It may well be related also to the Normande, a white lop-eared breed on the facing coast of

France which had been reduced to a population of only 126 sows and 27 boars by 1991. The Bayeux derived originally from crosses between the Normande and the Berkshire, is even more seriously endangered with only 18 sows and 6 boars. Other endangered local French breeds are the Limousine and the Basque, both lop-eared, black and white breeds, and the Gasconne, a lop-eared black breed similar in appearance to the Large Black. On the mainland of Europe, the Large Black was known as the Cornwall. In Germany in 1951 it comprised 1.4% of the pig population but had disappeared by 1983. Similarly, the Schwabisches-Hallisches Schwein (German Saddleback) could not be found in 1983 although it comprised 9.8% of the population in 1951.

Only a few local breeds have survived on the mainland of Europe. Apart from the French and the German breeds mentioned above, there are also the Black Iberic, Extremadura Red and Andalucian Spotted in Spain, the Alentejana in Portugal, the Cinta Senese, Casertana (Neapolitana), Mora Romagnola and Calabrese in Italy, the Bentheimer and Angeln Sattelschwein in Germany, and the Mangalitza in Hungary, in addition to others that may have survived in a relatively pure state in eastern Europe, together with Corsican, Sicilian, Sardinian and Greek feral populations.

## Poultry

The poultry industry has experienced explosive growth in the last fifty years. The trigger for this expansion was the rationing of red meat during and after World War II. The on-going success was due to the relative efficiency of genetic improvement programmes in a species with a short generation interval and a high reproductive rate. The result of these programmes was a remarkable increase in average performance, and a rapid shift towards specialisation.

Increasing specialisation led to the decline of the traditional dual-purpose breeds, and the development of hybrid breeding programmes by the large breeding companies resulted in the decline of all pure breeds. Reduction in population size caused a self-perpetuating cycle of increasingly intensive inbreeding and lower performance. The survival of the pure breeds lay in the hands of the exhibition breeders, but they are not constrained by the limitations of pure-breeding and their interest is motivated by the phenotypic characteristics of feather colour and comb type rather than by utility characteristics.

The large breeding companies are working with a very limited range of genetic material, although they claim to maintain thirty pure breeds in nucleus units, and they have observed and maintained variation within these breeds, although such variation usually relates only to a single-gene factor. However, this genetic material is not available to other breeders, and thus the global market for layers is controlled by less than ten primary breeders, by a similar number for broilers, and by only three for turkeys. This is an undesirable situation for four main reasons: it is imprudent that a major food resource should be controlled by a few major corporations; the reducing genetic base is likely at some stage to limit or prevent further improvement; the genetic vulnerability of monotypic populations has been demonstrated already with plant species; and the commercial strains of poultry are continually being selected for their suitability for controlled environment and battery cage systems.

Intensive systems of production are a relatively recent development. In 1946 less than one per cent of laying hens were kept in battery cages. By 1966 this had increased to sixty-five per cent, and now is in excess of ninety per cent. The increasing current public concern for animal welfare and for product quality is re-awakening interest in the old pure breeds. They are adapted to the more acceptable extensive systems of management, and the quality of their products is superior. The poultry programmes evolved and directed by Professor Roy Crawford at the University of Saskatchewan have provided the basis for systems for the identification of remaining stocks of the utility breeds, and for the formulation of breeding programmes which permit the maintenance of small closed populations without suffering the effects of in-breeding depression.

*Scots Dumpy: also known as Crawlers, Creepers and Bakies. At one time it was thought that they might have a role in battery-cage systems as less damage to eggs might be caused by short-legged birds*

In the U.K. eight breeds have initially attracted the attention of the Rare Breeds Survival Trust, namely the Scots Grey, Scots Dumpy, Old English Pheasant Fowl, Derbyshire Redcap, Dorking, Sussex, Cornish (Indian) Game and Croad Langshan. In addition it is likely that breeds such as Norfolk Black turkey, Brecon Buff goose and Aylesbury duck will be added in the future.

During the 18th century, there were two main lines of development in poultry breeding in Great Britain. In the North, the emphasis was on light breeds that were noted for their lack of broodiness and for their egg laying ability. In the South, the London market encouraged the development of a heavier, fatter bird where size and quality of flesh were more important.

The Old English Pheasant Fowl is typical of the northern type. Known previously as the Yorkshire Pheasant, it is a hardy, active bird that used to be a popular farmyard fowl. It was a good layer of white eggs but also had a meaty breast for its size. Cocks weigh 6–7 lb and hens 5–6lb. It occurs in two colour varieties, namely 'gold' (bay/red) and 'silver' (white with some markings) and has a rose comb.

The Derbyshire Redcap belongs to the same group. It is a outdoor fowl formerly noted as an excellent layer of white eggs with a broad, full meaty breast but the influence of fancy standards giving 45% of points on the show bench for head and comb, has hastened the decline of its utility characteristics and brought the breed to the verge of extinction. Cocks weigh 6–6.5 lb and hens 5–5.5 lb. The plumage is bay/red and it has a large rose comb.

The Scots Grey is also a light breed and it has been known in Scotland for more than 200 years. It is a non-sitting breed that lays a white egg. It has a deep, full breast that is very firm. Cocks weigh 7 lb, hens 5 lb. The plumage is cuckoo-feathered, the comb is single.

The Scots Dumpy is a related breed that differs in two important features. Firstly, it is an ideal sitter and broody mother and secondly it is short legged. Fowl with the short-leg (dumpy) characteristic were described as early as 1678.

The Dorking probably is the most ancient of the southern heavy breeds. It was described by the Roman writer Columella in AD 43 as robust and broad breasted and with five toes. In the early 19th century, birds of this type were found throughout southern England and were noted for their early eggs and abundant white flesh although they were rather smaller than the modern breed. The Dorking is now a massive-bodied, white-legged, tight-feathered bird primarily intended for the table although some strains are acceptable layers of tinted eggs. They are excellent foraging birds and consider leatherjackets a special delicacy. Cocks weigh 10–14 lb and hens 8–10 lb. There are

LEFT AND OPPOSITE:
*Croad Langshan and White Langshan cocks bred by Geoffrey Cloke, who transferred his recorded flock, established in 1878, to the Rare Breeds Survival Trust's Accredited Poultry Programme in 1993*

several colour varieties but the dark and the silver-grey have best retained the true quality of the breed.

The Sussex was developed from birds of Dorking type that existed as farm-yard fowl in the Weald. It is a true dual-purpose breed. Its deep, full body make it a good table bird while some strains have achieved outstanding results in laying trials with an annual production of more than 250 eggs. The hens are hardy and lay tinted eggs. There are several colour varieties and probably the red and the white are the most true to type. Cocks weigh 9 lb or more and hens 7 lb or more.

The Croad Langshan is not a native British breed. Langshan is a district in Northern China and birds from this area were imported by Major Croad in 1872 and fixed as a breed. It is a dual purpose breed; its size and high meat/bone ratio make it a good table bird while yields of 180 tinted eggs can be expected. The eggs previously were darker but some of the colour has been lost. The soft-feathered plumage is either black or white, the latter colour having arisen as a sport from the former. Cocks weigh 9 lb or more and hens 7 lb or more.

The Cornish Game (also known as Indian Game) has been bred in South West England since the early 19th century. It owes much of its ancestry to the Old English Game with influence from the Aseel. It has no equal for the abundant quantity and density of its breast meat and is a specialist table breed. It is broad and heavy boned with strong yellow legs and with extreme selection, may become too broad and wide-legged to mate naturally. Its crosses with early-maturing, white-fleshed, large breeds have played an important role in the broiler industry. Cocks weigh 8 lb or more and hens 6 lb or more.

The initial intention of the Rare Breeds Survival Trust was to establish its poultry programme on the model successfully demonstrated by Crawford, whereby four self-contained breeding units, each consisting of 50 hens, would effectively conserve the genetic material of a breed. The buzz

words of the Trust's programme were 'traditional', 'utility', 'welfare', 'environment' and 'quality'. The breeds included are long-established native British stock, and the birds are kept in non-intensive natural conditions. The combination of these genetic and environmental factors yields products of superior quality.

Birds were collected from as many sources as possible, but quickly it became evident that the loss of utility characteristics during the period of survival as 'fancy fowl' was greater than expected. Some flocks had been maintained in production units and it proved possible to establish accredited units for the Croad Langshan and White Langshan breeds from stock which had been in the ownership of Geoffrey Cloke's family since 1878; they achieved an average yield of almost 200 eggs per bird per year.

Similarly, White Sussex birds obtained from Geoffrey Marston and Geoffrey Cloke are from flocks that have demonstrated the ability of some birds to lay more than 250 eggs per year. However, other breeds were less successful and consequently the Trust has established small evaluation units to screen birds for utility characteristics as a preliminary step. In this way, it is hoped to restore the former egg-laying potential of breeds such as the Derbyshire Redcap and the Old English Pheasant Fowl. It is possible that inbreeding depression is the cause of the loss of production, but it is more likely that it is the natural result of the transfer of selection from utility to phenotypic characteristics.

The unusual Transylvanian Naked-Neck from Hungary and Romania has demonstrated its commercial credentials in two areas. Its lack of neck feathers enhances heat loss, a characteristic valued on small self-sufficiency units in hot parts of South Africa, while the diversion of dietary protein from feather growth to meat production has enabled the breed to contribute to broiler breeding programmes.

*Dexter cow with dwarf calf which shows the typical characteristics of a raised tailhead, short body, and relatively heavy head and fore-quarters*

## Congenital Defects

The commercial value of some breeds has suffered at various times through the occurrence of detrimental and even lethal genes. Clearly lethal genes are usually self-controlling in that their possessors do not survive to transmit them to another generation, but in some cases they have become an integral part of a breed's genotype, and they are especially dangerous in a minority breed. Pedigree breeders show an understandable reluctance to acknowledge the presence of a disease or genetic fault, which may consequently become widespread before the danger is fully appreciated.

Scrapie is a disease of the nervous system which has advanced under cover of this kind of secrecy. It is caused by an unidentified organism, possibly linked to bovine spongiform encephalopathy (BSE) and to Jacob Creutzfeld disease (premature senility) in humans, with a long incubation period that renders its control more difficult, and no cure is known. The disease has been known in Europe for several centuries, especially among Norfolk Horn sheep, and sporadic outbreaks have occurred in other parts of the world, where control has been attempted by a policy of compulsory slaughter. Infection is too widespread for this control to be exercised in Great Britain, but it is possible to select strains of sheep that are more resistant to the disease, as has been done in the Suffolk and Swaledale breeds, provided that the population is sufficiently large to permit heavy culling. It is now relatively easy to identify a fault in a minority breed, but the small size of the population and the limited number of bloodlines could make a drastic and immediate elimination of the defect a threat to the breed's existence, and more moderate methods must be employed to eradicate it.

This is the case with the dwarf defect in Dexter cattle, which is encouraged by the favour which has been bestowed on short-legged animals in the show ring. The dwarf factor is frequently given as an example of a partially dominant achondroplastic gene, which causes shortening of the bones and is lethal when both alleles are 'dwarf'. Calves conceived with the lethal condition are known as 'bulldogs' and are grossly deformed. It has been claimed that 25 per cent of Dexter calves are 'bulldogs', and are thus aborted; about 50 per cent are heterozygous dwarfs (i.e. Dexter); and about 25 per cent are longer-legged animals which are free from the defect, but are not acceptable as typical Dexters. This simplified explanation is no longer valid. My own observations have shown

*Hebridean ram. There are reports of multi-horned sheep in the Hebrides in the nineteenth century. The Hebridean is a primitive breed which shows a typical pattern of depressed winter metabolism, but which responds more than improved breeds to treatment with antisomatostatin which stimulates extra growth*

that there is a full graduation of type from extreme examples, exhibiting pronounced dwarf abnormalities, to animals which, although still small, are true miniatures of pleasing proportions without any unnatural features. The extreme dwarf type is only at one remove from the 'bulldog'. It may be identified by its short body and high tail-head, heavy head and forequarters, turned-out elbows and twisted fetlock joints, and a tendency to arthritis and dislocated stifle, as well as difficulties in conceiving and calving. Breeders who avoid cows with these characteristics are more likely to eliminate the 'bulldog' problem, and an increasing number of breeders are now adopting policies which will achieve this objective. Symes demonstrated that the average withers height of Dexter cows is 103.5 cm, while the average height of the dams of 'bulldog' calves was 99 cm. Dwarf-type cows have been favoured in the show ring, but it is conformation and type rather than withers height which is the best indication of the presence of the dwarf factor.

Some defects in rare breeds have been exposed by inbreeding. A particular family of Middle White sows, which have shorter snouts and nasal passages, suffer from lung problems because cold air is not properly warmed before entering the lungs. In an instance of particularly close breeding, atresia ani appeared in Whitefaced Woodland sheep, and a high proportion of inbred Cotswold sheep were affected by entropion. These and other defects are less severe in their effect than the 'bulldog' gene, but they may be equally difficult to eradicate in a minority breed. A problem such as screwtail in Portland sheep, caused by the fusion of one or more pairs of the coccygeal vertebrae at the end of the tail, is of no significance and can safely be ignored. On the other hand, a condition known as 'split eyelid' can be more serious. It is found in multihorned sheep, such as the Manx Loghtan and Hebridean of Scandinavian origin and the Jacob and Navajo-Churro of Iberian origin. The defect is closely linked to the polycerate characteristic, and I have never seen it in a two-horned sheep. (The term 'polycerate' has become established by long usage. It was first used by Low 150 years ago, but the more correct term would be 'polycornute'.) An affected eyelid does not give proper protection to the eye, and the long hairs which tend to grow from the abnormal area often cause further irritation. The damage may be as slight as a 'weepy' eye or as drastic as complete blindness. It can be progressively eliminated by selection within a breed, and it appears to have a lower incidence among Manx Loghtan sheep than among Jacob and Hebridean sheep.

The most common problems encountered with all species of domestic livestock are those associated with reduced fertility or even complete sterility. These may stem from disease factors, such as

the many abortion organisms which can be controlled by management procedures, but inherited defects are a more difficult obstacle. The many and varied causes include gonadal hypoplasia, undescended testicles, cystic ovaries, inability or unwillingness to copulate, chromosomal translocation, and dystocia. Gonadal hypoplasia (underdeveloped sex organs) is a strongly inherited condition. In the polled Swedish Mountain breed of cattle, two show-winning bulls, each with one hypoplastic and one normal testicle, almost ruined the breed by producing subfertile female progeny. Similarly, a monorchid male (with one normal testicle) is able to breed and so transmit the defect of cryptorchidism, in which the testes do not descend from the abdominal cavity into the scrotum. There is a surprising level of monorchidism among the primitive breeds of sheep. During the survey of sheep carried out in 1977 on the island of Linga Holm, ten (9.2 per cent) of the 109 North Ronaldsay ram lambs examined had a monorchid condition, while two (1.8 per cent) were cryptorchid and thus infertile.

The presence of ovarian cysts may be manifested in nymphomania and can be inherited through either sire or dam. A survey of Simmental cattle in 1954 showed that one bull had sired forty-seven daughters, of which twenty-eight developed cystic ovaries after the first or second calving. The selection of breeding stock which exhibit strong sexual character is an important factor in maintaining high fertility. Breeding from feminine-type bulls can lead to reduced sexual vigour and a lack of interest in the opposite sex, as some buyers of very expensive prize-winning bulls have discovered.

Chromosomal translocation, in which chromosomes are misplaced, may be a further cause of reduced fertility. An instance of a chromosomal aberration (1/29 Robertsonian translocation) in Swedish Red-and-White cattle resulted in a significant drop in fertility. The same defect is widespread in the British White breed, and in 1975 had an average frequency of 42 per cent, with 64 per cent of the animals being carriers. By 1988, on the basis of fifty-seven animals tested, the frequency of the gene had risen to 50 per cent, and 73.7 per cent of the animals were carriers of the defect. It has not been possible at this stage to determine beyond any doubt whether this aberration is related to the infertility noted in the British White, but a connection seems likely. The defect has been recorded in more than twenty breeds in many parts of the world, including Charolais, Simmental, Grey Steppe, and particularly Romagnola. In native British breeds it has only been found in the British White and, at a lower level, in the Red Poll and Irish Moiled. It may be significant that these three breeds have been influenced by recent importations from Scandinavia:

the British White by two Fjallras bulls imported in 1949, the Red Poll by the importation of Red Dane cattle in 1961, and the Irish Moiled by a Polled Finnish bull, Hakku, in 1950. The pedigree of Hakku (born 4.3.49; HB No. 2118) is known: his sire was Otus (72) and his dam was Harne (313J), but there are no records of any tests for the defect in these animals.

Several other defects of cattle have been introduced into Great Britain by imported livestock. A deficiency of the clotting agent Factor XI causing haemophilia, a heritable enzyme deficiency known as DUMPS, which causes unthriftiness, early abortion and sometimes death, an enzyme deficiency which affects the immune system (BLAD), and Mulefoot, were all brought in from North America, while Snoeken Bek (overshot jaw, pike nose) came from Holland. As these defects generally seem to be controlled by recessive genes, they can filter surreptitiously into the native population, and this reinforces the importance of maintaining the purity of rare breeds of all species, and not permitting grading-up programmes.

Some of the defects mentioned above can be identified by visual inspection of the animal, while others demand blood-typing analysis, progeny testing, or other specialist techniques. Dystocia, or difficult parturition, is a problem which can be identified and prevented in several ways. The bull used has a marked effect on calf mortality and the incidence of difficult calvings. We have already seen that several of the large breeds from the mainland of Europe, such as the Charolais, Italian White breeds, Belgian Blue and Maine-Anjou, can cause severe problems. In contrast, calves sired by breeds such as the White Park and Longhorn are not only born without difficulty but are active and vigorous from birth, and these results continue to be confirmed to me by reports from commercial cattle breeders. The breed of the dam also affects the incidence of dystocia. In research funded by the Rare Breeds Survival Trust it was shown that the incidence was higher among Friesian, British White and Dexter cows than among Shetland, Longhorn, White Park and Kerry cows, and that the critical factor is the relationship of pelvic dimension to body size. Straight hocks in cows of any breed tend to be accompanied by a square, level rump, with a pelvic opening of reduced size, and this can exaggerate any calving problems. A cow with a sloping pelvic girdle and lower pin bones is less likely to experience calving difficulties.

*Comparison of Ease of Parturition in Five Breeds of Cattle*

| Breed | Number of sires used | Number of calvings | Difficult calvings (%) | Cows | | | |
| | | | | Girth (cm) | Withers height (cm) | Rump Length (cm) | Hip width (cm) |
|---|---|---|---|---|---|---|---|
| British White | 11 | 72 | 6.9 | 193.6 | 128.5 | 55.1 | 57.5 |
| Friesian | 10 | 647 | 6.2 | 204.6 | 134.8 | 54.8 | 59.2 |
| Dexter | 17 | 264 | 5.3 | 157.7 | 100.7 | 42.9 | 43.2 |
| White Park | 9 | 63 | NIL | 200.1 | 130.5 | 56.0 | 57.8 |
| Shetland | — | 62 | NIL | 183.8 | 121.2 | 51.1 | 55.1 |

The production of live offspring must be the prime consideration in any evaluation of relative commercial merits, and the minority breeds, which have been required to survive and reproduce without close supervision, have a decided advantage in this respect. There is an academic philosophy which argues that defects should not be eliminated because they are part of the genotype of a breed, but this argument carries little weight with either practical breeders or pragmatic conservationists.

# CHAPTER 7

# A STRATEGY FOR
# GENETIC CONSERVATION

OPPOSITE:

*Longhorn bull, Garrick, bred by Robert Fowler of Little Rollright in Oxfordshire in the late eighteenth century from stock bred by Bakewell and Webster of Canley, from a painting attributed to J. Boultbee*

ABOVE:

*Two-pounder, a famous Dishley Leicester ram, from a painting by J. Digby Curtis 1790*

## An Alien Philosophy

The title of 'master breeder' is awarded sparingly. It conjures up the image of a genius who excels in the art of applied genetics, or whose sophisticated techniques have revolutionised a significant aspect of livestock production, but it is difficult in reality to find adequate evidence of originality in the methods employed by those who might be master breeders. Robert Bakewell, who is extolled by many agricultural commentators as the founder of animal breeding methods for his work with Longhorn cattle, Leicester sheep and Shire horses in the eighteenth century, benefited from the earlier work of other breeders and applied techniques that were already in common use among breeders of Thoroughbred horses. It was the vast scale of Kleberg's farming enterprise in Texas that enabled him to exploit chance improvements that arose in his cattle and to promote his new breed, the Santa Gertrudis, in the first half of the twentieth century. The qualification shared by Bakewell and Kleberg was not their skill as animal breeders, but rather their ability to

*Milking Devon cow of the old type in Massachusetts in 1975*

appreciate the requirements of a changing market and to popularise their product. Bakewell understood the significance of the Industrial Revolution and was sufficiently astute to perceive an increasing market for fat, early-maturing livestock. Kleberg realised the basic unfitness of European breeds of livestock for the Texan climate and, in the absence of the Texas Longhorn which had been discarded earlier, simply introduced cattle of Zebu origin to provide heat tolerance.

In both cases breeders were taking positive action. The philosophy of genetic conservation, on the other hand, is based on the apparently negative concept of maintaining the status quo, and that is what is so difficult for many scientists and livestock breeders to understand. The idea is alien to the general tenets of livestock production, and conflict between the principle of conserving genetic variability and the instinctive urge to improve – or more accurately to change – is an accepted feature of the conservation of rare breeds.

The search for improvement, or change, can take many forms, but in the context of an orthodox breed structure, usually represented by a Breed Society, people's aims will often emerge as one of two extremes, which might be described as 'reactionary' or 'progressive'. When reactionary attitudes and self-interest prevail in a Breed Council they result in an image of an animal which is embodied in the Breed Standards and becomes an unchangeable ideal. This rigid specification of type allows none of the variation and flexibility that is the essence of livestock improvement. If the objectives of all breeders were to coincide completely all progress would cease, because the possibility of adapting to the requirements of a changing environment or different market demands would be precluded by the uniformity of the animals. The reactionary approach has, on occasions, reached ridiculous proportions. For example, red-and-white cattle were excluded by the British Friesian Cattle Society from the Herd Book purely on the grounds of colour, despite the claim of the red-and-white cattle to pedigrees as unimpeachable as those of the black-and-white cattle – a prime example of the unhealthy obsession with colour that has been noted in respect of many breeds. Pressure towards uniformity results in the continual elimination of genetic material – a kind of voluntary stripping of assets.

Bakewell and Kleberg are among the progressive breeders at the other end of the scale. They are not bound by the limits of within-breed selection; the purity of existing breeds holds no special significance for them. Bakewell's Dishley Leicester sheep were not patiently evolved from the native sheep of the county but, rather, they were urgently forced by the addition of qualities from the longwools of Lincoln and the shortwools of Hereford. Kleberg stirred Brahman, Shorthorn and Hereford into his Santa Gertrudis brew, probably adding a dash of Afrikander for good meas-

*Llandinabo Lingo, a genuine pure Hereford bull, bred by Major Michael Symonds in the heartland of the breed from Vern foundation stock. The traditional Hereford, like the Angus and some other native British breeds, is now almost an endangered type owing to heavy infiltration by imported stock of questionable ancestry*

ure. While this may be exciting stuff, such rapid progress poses an even greater threat to genetic conservation than the gentle drifting that results from reactionary attitudes. Crossing a breed immediately halves the original genetic material, and subsequent stages can dilute it further. If breeds are numerically strong the effect of such a policy on the total population may be limited; but if Gloucester cattle, with less than 400 cows, were to be crossed with the similarly marked but unrelated Pinzgau, it would result in the Gloucester's effective elimination as an identifiable entity and, consequently, the irretrievable loss of genetic material.

Between the sacrifice of genetic characteristics in the pursuit of greater uniformity within a closed population, on one hand, and replacement of the original qualities in crossbreeding programmes on the other, there is a middle course in which the conservationists can take the best and discard the worst elements of each extreme. In an ideal situation, they would maintain a breed as a closed population, but would organise selection and mating procedures to ensure the maximum variation within the population. In this way the purity and distinctive character of the breed is protected while its options remain as wide as possible in order to take full advantage of changing circumstances.

In practice, the philosophies defined here as distinct alternatives almost lose their separate identities among the complexities of pedigree stock, pure-bred unregistered stock, crossbred stock and mongrelised stock. It is clear, moreover, that whatever the pace-setters may determine regarding any change in type or function of a breed, a few breeders will continue to maintain the 'old' type when it is no longer fashionable, and unwittingly make an invaluable contribution to genetic conservation. But there is a time limit to this source of original stock. These breeders tend to fall outside the confines of their Breed Society, and are forced to use fashionable registered bulls to continue breeding their stock. We have an example in the change in the type of Devon – the Red Ruby cattle native to the South-West of England. The original Devon was of some importance as a triple-purpose breed and its milk made the county famous for its clotted cream. Now the Devon is a specialist beef breed, and no animals of the old type remain in Britain, although a few have been located in Massachusetts where they are being carefully monitored. A recent decision by British breeders to accept crosses with the Salers breed as eligible for registration has undermined further the value of the pure breed.

The source of the problem lies in the hierarchical structure of breeding common to most breeds in developed countries, where fashion and speculation are powerful motives. In this system a number of herds, or even a single herd, can exert a powerful influence on the remainder of the breed. The Vern herd under the ownership of the late Captain R. S. de Quincey at Marden in

Herefordshire, became the ideal of Hereford breeders in all parts of the world, and Vern bulls dominated pedigrees throughout the breed. Likewise, the Terling and Lavenham herds established a position of pre-eminence among British Friesians, largely through the reputation of the imported bull, Terling Marthus, which A. Robertson and A. A. Asker calculated in 1951 had 'contributed 6 per cent of the genes in the breed and is therefore virtually the great-great-grandfather of the breed'.

This typical breed structure (described as pyramidal stratification) integrates breeders who vary in attitude, ability and resources into a single operational unit. The pyramid must have a strong foundation of commercial herds containing crossbred derivatives of the pure-bred stock from the higher strata. The pure-bred herds are divided into those which register only female stock, those which rely mainly on the sale of crossing bulls, and those which provide bulls for pedigree breeding. The later, élite category effectively determines the future direction of the breed, and the figure below illustrates how less than 10 per cent of the registered herds supply half the bulls in the breed.

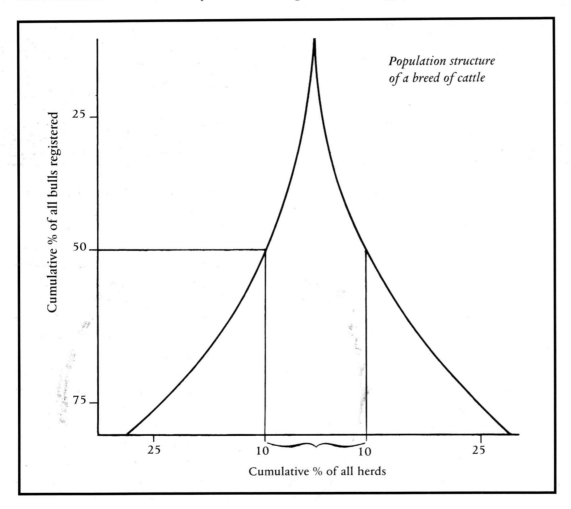

*Population structure of a breed of cattle*

The numerically small breeds possess the same structure, although when very few herds are concerned the pyramid is less clearly defined. One of the oldest herds of British White cattle was the Somerford herd owned by Sir Walter Shakerly in Cheshire and established some time around 1725. It was dispersed in 1925, only five years after the breed's first Herd Book was published, but nevertheless Somerford bulls or their sons were used in all except two of the herds listed in the first volumes of the book and featured very strongly in the Faygate and Woodbastwick herds, which were themselves near the apex of the breed pyramid. Thus for good or ill the fortunes of the British White were shaped largely by Sir Walter Shakerly's ideals for the breed. That these ideals embraced the use of other breeds, such as Shorthorn, Galloway and White Park, is only of academic interest as far as the British White is concerned. It is consigned to history, but it is a clear demon-

TOP: *Portland ram with ewes at the National Agricultural Centre. The ewe on the right is polled, and this may have been the result of crossbreeding in the flock at Calke Abbey*

ABOVE: *The author with Bona, a Pyrenean Mountain guard dog at the CS Fund farm in California*

stration of the ever-present danger of a hierarchical breed structure whether it is maintained alone or combined with 'progressive' crossbreeding or 'reactionary' self-interest.

The show ring has helped to accentuate the effect of the hierarchical structure and tends to give fashion a higher priority than commercial characteristics. This is best illustrated by poultry breeds where 'fancy' breeders have no inhibitions or scruples regarding the introduction of outside blood to achieve the desired feather colour or comb shape, although this has been at the expense of the utility characteristics. Both Border Leicester and Bluefaced Leicester sheep have suffered from the undue attention paid to the shape of their Roman nose rather than their prolificacy and milk yield; shortwool breeds disguise their true qualities beneath a carefully carded, trimmed and shaped fleece; and most breeds of all species are presented in the show ring in an overfinished condition rather than in 'working trim'. The show ring influence probably is seen at its extreme in the Kennel Club standards, with breeds such as the Bulldog, Basset Hound, Old English Sheepdog and St Bernard no longer fit for their original purpose, but the warning signs are there for other species.

Some dog breeds are still working animals, although even they are not entirely immune from the predations of the Kennel Clubs. The shepherding dogs are likely to retain their true function as long as there are flocks of sheep, but an encouraging reversal to working life has been seen with the large, guard-dog breeds. These are not herding dogs, but rather travel with the flocks patrolling and protecting them. The Anatolian Karabash (literally 'black head – dark mask) is a typical example. A powerful, athletic animal, a mature dog weighs c.140 lb and stands 32 inches at the shoulder. It originated in Turkey, but now is found working in North America and Australasia. Other valuable breeds of this type are the Pyreneean Mountain dog and the Hungarian Komondor.

The Rare Breeds Survival Trust has attempted to counter-balance this influence by introducing a system of card-grading. This system has been used since the mid-1980s and has been demonstrated at a series of workshops by the author with a Portland breeder, Frank Bailey. Each animal is awarded a card denoting 'Above average', 'Average' or 'Below average', compared with show classes where all the attention is focused on the animal which is awarded the top prize card. Card-grading is an evaluation of the genetic quality of the animal, whereas judging at Shows evaluates the ability of the owner to condition and present the exhibit and to disguise its defects.

## A Prototype

By the mid-twentieth century, with the minor breeds in peril of extinction, there was a serious need for a programme of genetic conservation that was uncluttered by the preconceptions of orthodox livestock breeding. The clean sheet on which principles and methods could be mapped out existed in very few places. Countries with undeveloped and unexploited livestock populations provided one possible base, and Mason's FAO report on the Kuri cattle of Lake Chad gives a valuable blueprint for safeguarding indigenous and largely untouched breeds.

In developed countries, it is hard to find breeds which not only represent an original type but have remained relatively pure. Because the whole process of development over a period of many centuries has been a continuing process of hybridisation and inbreeding, out of a total of more than a hundred large breeds of livestock in the British Isles only breeds such as Soay and North Ronaldsay sheep, Chillingham and Kerry cattle, and Exmoor ponies can realistically claim any comparison with Kuri cattle. Neither the Soay nor the North Ronaldsay breeds had been controlled by a Flock Book Society. The Soay had been generally regarded as a wild animal, and the North Ronaldsay was supervised on its native island by a Sheep Court concerned with ownership and management of the sheep rather than pedigree records. Here then was an opportunity to demonstrate, in the midst of a sophisticated and highly developed livestock industry, that genetic conservation was a serious business, not incompatible with commercial practice but complementary to it. In 1974 a registration programme was established by Michael Rosenberg and myself through Countrywide Livestock Ltd for ten breeds of sheep that did not have existing registration facilities: Soay, North Ronaldsay, Shetland, Manx Loghtan, Hebridean, Castlemilk Moorit, Portland, Norfolk Horn, Whitefaced Woodland and Cotswold. Volume I of this *Combined Flock Book* was published in 1975 and contained entries from sixty-five breeders. By Volume XIV in 1989 there were 558 breeders registering 4465 lambs. As soon as the programme was launched there was a risk of its falling into the traditional Breed Society mould, but any such possibilities were forestalled by the statement of intent in the preface to Volume II, which made quite clear that it was 'not intended to impose rigid type specifications which can only act to the detriment of each breed'.

Although the *Combined Flock Book* was established as a conservation exercise, its potential value is much wider. The use of a central office to co-ordinate the administration of several breeds spreads overhead costs more thinly, and when the system had been proven and computerised it was possible to offer it as a service to other breeds and Breed Societies.

The *Combined Flock Book* embodies the two basic principles of genetic conservation: purity of descent and the maintenance of genetic variability. As a prototype it represents a vital step forward. It has projected rare breeds onto the national scene, and is represented on the Council of the National Sheep Association. It has promoted the view that variability is more desirable than extreme uniformity. For example, within traditional Flock Book regulations the Soay might have been standardised to one colour, but the *Combined Flock Book* embraces the whole range of colours recognised in the breed. The colour is irrelevant as long as the purity of the animal is not in question. It is necessary to distinguish between unusual colours which arise from natural variation within a breed, and those which are evidence of recent crossbreeding. In the 1980s white 'Hebridean' sheep have been recorded, and have formed a breed association (Seann Innse'gall), but they have been disbarred from the *Combined Flock Book* because white should not appear in a breed where the true colour is recessive black. It is likely, therefore, that some recent crossing with the Black Welsh Mountain or maybe the Jacob (dominant black) took place, as it did in the early twentieth century as reported by H. J. Elwes. Likewise, Manx Loghtan sheep with white markings are disqualified as moorit has been the established colour of the breed for eighty years. An evaluation of the genetic purity of an animal may be complex. For example, a black Portland is not eligible for registration in the *Combined Flock Book*, but when the Calke Abbey flock was presented en bloc for registration in 1990 many factors had to be considered. Anecdotal and recorded

*Shetland cow being milked by a crofter. Sixty years ago the cattle of this breed were of various colours, but only black-and-white calves found a ready market in Aberdeen, and from the mid-1930s the other colours disappeared. During the Second World War, the subsidy for beef calves was not paid for pure Shetland calves, and this encouraged breeders to adopt crossbreeding programmes*

evidence of crossing forty years previously had to be evaluated together with recent biochemical analyses and phenotypic assessments of dark pigment.

There is a difficulty in diverting the attention of breeders from the purely visual characteristics, such as colour, to the subtler, more important qualities that are becoming evident to keepers of these breeds. It is proving equally difficult to distract geneticists from their concentration on immediate commercial considerations to a view of long-term benefits. One of the foremost pig geneticists of the present day suffers from this problem. In a private communication in 1975, he wrote:

> From the present day agricultural viewpoint it is difficult to anticipate any future function for any of these breeds [i.e. minor breeds in Great Britain]. The rate of improvement in breeds such as the Large White and Landrace is such that the commercial attributes of untested breeds falls further and further behind. Use of genes from these breeds, even in small proportions, then becomes increasingly difficult. My own view – which is a minority one – is that there would be advantage in creating a gene pool from these distinct breeds and selecting it intensively for commercial attributes. In this way one could create a reserve population which could be drawn upon for needs which are not at present anticipated. It is true that the process of pooling the breeds makes the extraction of useful genes more difficult but one has to set this against the narrowing of the improvement lag which I think is important if conserved breeds are to be used in the future.

This logic cannot be disputed if we accept his basic premise, but there is no guarantee that the present-day agricultural viewpoint will remain. There are already signs that current intensive systems of pig production may turn out to have been an expensive diversion down a cul-de-sac, while the superior meat quality of the rare breeds refutes his entire argument.

This is the heart of the problem. The minor breeds must not be forced into the patterns designed for currently fashionable breeds. A Kerry cannot compete with a British Friesian purely for milk production; a Soay is not in the same league as a British Milksheep for prolificacy and milk yield; and it would take many generations of intensive selection to reduce the thickness of backfat on the Middle White to Landrace standards. We do not expect them to outpace the popular breeds in their specialities. Instead, our concern should be to identify the important qualities of the minor breeds and, having done so, to match their characteristics with a system of production that enhances their value. There is no cause for the owners of any breed to feel defensive; they should instead be prepared to exercise positive thinking. It is for the minor breeds to find their own niche within the livestock industry.

Once we have accepted the importance of positive-thinking breeders, it is only realistic to concede that each individual will be motivated by his own ideals and objectives to a great extent, even within as idealistic a project as the *Combined Flock Book* programme of registration. Some breeders, because of personality, publicity or foresight, will assume a dominant position and exert a significant influence on the whole breed. We must accept that Man's ambition and one of its consequences, the hierarchical breed structure, wield greater strength than abstract concepts, but nevertheless a high proportion of the foundation animals registered in the *Combined Flock Book* are still represented in the current crop of lambs. Thus the registration programme was a development of historic importance, and it was reinforced in Great Britain by a wide range of projects undertaken by various interested organisations, among which the Rare Breeds Survival Trust holds a prominent position.

The strategy of genetic conservation must take account of the future. It cannot limit itself simply to preservation but must include evaluation of the endangered breeds and a search for ways in which they might be utilised beneficially. The main justification for conserving domestic livestock is the chance that their qualities will have some value later on. A continuing programme is required to identify and define those qualities.

## Semen, Ova and Embryos

Perhaps the most important and ambitious project undertaken by the Rare Breeds Survival Trust was the creation of a Semen Bank. In view of the potential ability of artificial insemination to reduce the genetic base of a breed, or as a commodity of international trade to overwhelm native breeds with semen from exotic breeds, it may seem strange that the Trust should set such a high priority on their Semen Bank project, but normal rules do not necessarily apply when the numbers of a breed fall below the safety level. One of the most important reasons why cows and sows of the minority breeds are not used for pure-breeding is the unavailability of a bull or boar. The Department of Agriculture and Fisheries for Scotland appreciated the problem in isolated areas and established at Inverness a stud of Shetland bulls that were made available to the crofters in the Shetland Islands.

In some cases, other factors are important. Paradoxically, the good qualities of a breed may contribute to its decline through crossbreeding. The maternal qualities of Shetland cows were so highly regarded in their native islands that they were in great demand for crossing with fleshy Beef Shorthorn and Aberdeen Angus bulls. As a result, fewer and fewer Shetland cows were bred pure until the breed reached its present critical position. That a breed should become endangered because it lacks the qualifications to compete in a hard commercial world is an easy argument to grasp, but there seems little justice when its capacity for commercial success leads to the same endpoint. This applies to very few breeds, however. Apart from Shetland cattle, we might list the Irish Dun, a number of native pony breeds which have been seriously infiltrated by Arab blood, and some of the coloured pig breeds which have been crossed with white boars to produce hardy crossbred sows.

Among the various reasons for crossbreeding, the unavailability of a suitable male is the most common. When a breed is low in numbers the average size of the component breeding units is correspondingly reduced, often falling below the number of females with which it is economically realistic to keep a male. When the Gloucester Cattle Herd Book was reformed in 1973, a total of fifty-eight cows and heifers were spread around twenty-two herds, of which only three contained more than five cows and heifers. In normal circumstances, none of these herds would have kept a bull but, fortunately, there is always an abundance of enthusiasm in a newly formed organisation, and the members of the emergent Gloucester Cattle Society managed to muster a total of twelve bulls. In one case a herd consisted on one cow and two bulls – a sure recipe for bovine frustration! However, such situations were unreliable, and the Semen Bank was established to give greater security to such endangered breeds of cattle.

The initial moves were made by the Milk Marketing Board of England and Wales. As early as 1969, in announcing the creation of the Museum Bank, Dr Kevin O'Connor, then head of the Board's Animal Breeding Division and later Managing Director of Farm Services, stated the case very clearly:

> All breeds of cattle are changing all the time and it seems a good idea to preserve the genetic variation that exists so that at any time in the future we can go back to it. Thirty years ago many of our beef breeds had a lot more size; then they were bred smaller and neater; now we are trying to get the size back in them again. It might have saved us a lot of time today if we had been able to go to the store and get some semen from a rough Hereford of the early 1900s. We can never be absolutely certain that we are breeding the right type of cattle. Tastes may change. People might want more fat on their beef or less fat in their milk.

The Milk Marketing Board and the Rare Breeds Survival Trust joined forces in this project, and semen has been stored from more than 200 bulls. The Trust selects the bulls and draws up an agreement with the owner, who is responsible for isolating the bull, obtaining the appropriate licence, and arranging for testing. The Trust, for its part, meets the cost of these services, transports the bull to the Centre and pays the owner a lump sum. From about 300 straws of semen collected from each bull, 100–150 are stored in the long-term Semen Banks and the remainder are available for purchase by breeders, or are used by the Trust in contract mating schemes or in specific projects designed to obtain more information on the breeds. Semen from less endangered breeds is also obtained, but only from bulls that are of genuine original type and this is an urgent programme as the rate of introgression would seem to be increasing. Several of these breeds, including the Devon, Sussex, Lincoln Red and South Devon, are being modified by crossing with continental beef breeds, such as the Limousin, Maine-Anjou and Salers. For example, in 1987 both the male and female Lincoln Red Champion at the Lincolnshire Show carried a 12½ per cent infusion of Maine-Anjou blood. The evidence of some black Chianina look-alikes of Canadian origin, would suggest that the process of 'genetic pollution' has extended already to the Angus which is not yet seriously endangered.

The principles underlying the selection of bulls to be included in the Semen Bank are that they must be a good representative sample of the contemporary breed, and that there must be semen available from sufficient bulls to provide an adequate choice for breeders and to maintain genetic variation and prevent inbreeding. The target is to collect semen from twenty-five unrelated bulls in each breed, and to repeat this at five-generation intervals. The bulls are selected following a computer analysis of breed structure, and where necessary a contract mating policy is followed and bull-rearing incentives are provided. This target often is not met, but the limit is determined not by the Trust's programme but by the small number of bloodlines and the limited number of suitable bulls that are available. The table sets out the number of sire lines that can be identified in some minor breeds, but even these lines may be related one or two generations further back.

*Sire Lines of Some Minority Cattle Breeds*

| Breed | No. of sire lines | Foundation bulls of each line |
|---|---|---|
| Gloucester | 3 | Wickcourt Gloucester, Wickcourt Bovril, Batthurst Brewer. |
| North Dairy Shorthorn | 3 | Hartley Fold Duke, Undercragg Overlord, Prince. |
| Shetland | 4 | Glebe Rasmie, Heather Chieftan, Knocknagael Donald, Knocknagael Rory. |
| White Park | 3 | Dynevor Penparc, Whipsnade 201, Woburn Pykent 19. |

Most countries that have implemented a rare breeds conservation programme have included semen collection and storage as a high priority. In both the UK and France the semen is divided between long-term storage and current use.

*Semen from rare breeds of cattle stored in U.K. and France (No. of bulls) 1992*

| | United Kingdom | | | France | |
| Breed | For AI and storage | For storage only | Breed | For AI and storage | For storage only |
| --- | --- | --- | --- | --- | --- |
| Beef Shorthorn* | 3 | 2 | Amoricaine | 5 | 8 |
| British White* | 1 | 7 | Auroise | 13 | 0 |
| Gloucester | 12 | 2 | Bearnaise | 10 | 0 |
| Irish Moiled | 5 | 3 | Bretonne Pie Noire | 17 | 4 |
| Kerry* | 6 | 5 | Ferrandaise | 16 | 0 |
| Red Poll* | 0 | 12 | Froment du Léon | 8 | 0 |
| Shetland | 12 | 3 | Gasconne Areolee | 7 | 0 |
| Vaynol | 6 | 0 | Lourdaise | 9 | 0 |
| White Park | 14 | 4 | Maraichine | 3 | 2 |
| | | | Nantaise | 3 | 0 |
| | | | Villard de Lans | 15 | 0 |

* Extra semen also stored by the Breed Society

The potential dangers of an A.I. policy are demonstrated within the success of the programme of the MMB. The MMB carried out more than 43 million first inseminations in only its first thirty-three years, and the dominance of certain bulls in an operation on this scale poses a real threat to genetic variability. For example, the Friesian bull Alsopdale Sunbeam 2nd, who was born in 1964 and died in 1979, produced over 424,000 doses of semen, and by the end of September 1979 had provided 214,293 first inseminations. Similarly, Holmland Adema, who died in July 1977 at the age of 13½ years, sired more than 188,000 calves, while his contemporary Trengwainton Guardian exerted an even greater influence on the Guernsey breed. Increasingly sophisticated sire evaluation techniques in the popular breeds are likely to concentrate breeding programmes on an ever-reducing genetic base. Taken to extremes, such a situation could have an adverse effect even on the ubiquitous Friesian–Holstein; the danger to numerically small breeds is proportionately greater. In setting up the Semen Bank the Trust was aware of these dangers. It took upon itself the responsibility of ensuring that all the existing bloodlines within a breed were maintained; if a line became weaker, it was supported and strengthened; if a line became dominant, it was controlled. Once again there was possible conflict between conservationists' long-term ideals and breeders' immediate dreams.

Initially the Semen Bank was limited to cattle, but in 1987 it was extended to include pigs, and it is planned to extend it further to include sheep and goats. The Trust carries out an annual Bull Fertility Survey to calculate the conception rates achieved with the semen. In some cases low conception rates are the fault of low-fertility semen, but in most cases they result from the inability of owners to detect heat periods in their cows accurately.

The storage of frozen semen and the use of artificial insemination lead on naturally to the storage of frozen embryos and the use of embryo-transfer as techniques of genetic conservation. While the semen represents only half of a potential new animal, an embryo is a complete and independent unit. When a female mammal is born, the ovaries already contain about 100,000 immature ova which, in normal circumstances, are shed in very small numbers at regular intervals after puberty, so that the supply is never used up. It is possible with suitable hormone treatment to increase the number of ova released and transfer each ovum after fertilisation to another female. Dr Christopher Polge at Cambridge has also developed the technique of post-mortem recovery of ova for *in vitro* culture to maturity and *in vitro* fertilisation. These techniques make possible the production of many more progeny than with natural breeding procedures, and a group of relatively inexpensive crossbred cows can rear *in utero* the potentially valuable calves of an élite Simmental or rare Irish Moiled cow.

However, the risk must be clearly worthwhile before one of the fifty or so Irish Moiled cows is committed to such a programme; the increase in production of calves must outweigh the danger of losing a breeding cow. It is not easy to calculate the number of extra calves that might be obtained, as the efficiency of different operating theatres varies widely and procedures are being continually improved, especially with the introduction of non-surgical techniques. An experienced team can recover on average 6–7 viable embryos per collection from a normal cow, and 60 per cent of these might result in a pregnancy.

In a breed with a small population, there is an increased chance of the loss of genetic material by the selection of preferred types by breeders, by inbreeding, and by genetic drift. These effects can be reduced by using a very high ratio of males, or possibly by random breeding, but such policies are not acceptable to breeders. Thus it is essential to complement the maintenance of live populations with the storage of frozen semen and embryos. These serve as an insurance, both against a change of type or function within the breed, and against the possible extinction of the live population. As with semen, embryos should be collected at five-generation intervals, with twenty-five cows each providing twenty-five embryos for storage.

Beyond embryo-transfer we move into the field of genetic engineering. Research is far advanced into techniques for 'sexing' semen and embryos, and for microsurgical procedures for splitting embryos to produce clones. Single-parent cloning is a reality in some species, as is the transfer of nuclei from early development embryos to unfertilised eggs. Transgenic techniques, by the direct injection of DNA copies of desired genes into an egg shortly after fertilisation, give further opportunity for genetic manipulation and genetic 'improvement'. Sex selection, the isolation and cloning of specific genes, the production of embryonic stem cells, and the mapping of animal genomes are all possible. Genetic engineering, taken to its logical conclusion, could make genetic conservation through the medium of rare breeds unnecessary. However, that is a long way ahead and in the short term genetic engineering and the analysis of genetic markers is more likely to prove of value in saving rare breeds and rare alleles. Our concern should be with more mundane and urgent matters. An ongoing problem, and one that can easily be intensified by the use of the advanced techniques just described, is that of inbreeding.

## Inbreeding

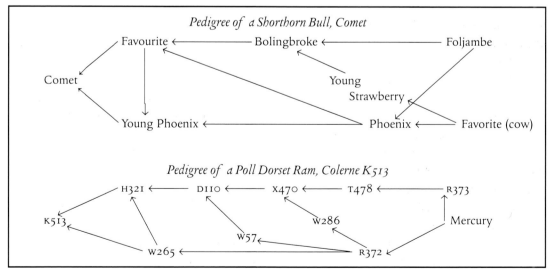

Inbreeding is not necessarily undesirable. It is viewed with concern in some circles because it lifts the lid off a genetic Pandora's box, exposing defects that lurk in recessive corners of the genotypes. It is the genotype that is at fault, not the inbreeding, and the majority of successful animal breeders have inbred at some stage in their programme, to great effect in many instances. Charles Colling

*Shorthorn bull, Comet, sold by Charles Colling at the Ketton Sale in 1810 for 1000 guineas, from a painting by Thomas Weaver*

used extreme inbreeding to produce Comet, the outstanding Shorthorn bull sold for 1000 guineas in 1810. I used similar techniques in my Colerne flock of *Poll Dorset* sheep to achieve performance levels 32.5 per cent above breed average and 17 per cent higher than the next best flock. Comet and K513 had inbreeding coefficients of 46.87 per cent and 30.47 per cent respectively, whereas most breeders would consider 12.5 per cent to be their upper limit.

Inbreeding is regularly quoted in textbooks of animal breeding as a cause of reductions in performance, vigour and viability. In some cases this is true, but many livestock advisers oppose its use without clearly understanding its potential value. Some breeds have passed through a bottle-neck of inbreeding without obvious harm, and some families of domestic livestock can tolerate high levels of inbreeding without revealing genetic skeletons in their cupboards. In such cases, inbreeding can be used to advantage to concentrate the desirable qualities of a good bloodline. The herd of White Park cattle at Whipsnade, which was dispersed in 1973, contained some examples of very close breeding. Whipsnade 288 provides an extreme case, as the result of mating a cow to her own son, who was in turn the product of a father–daughter union. Whipsnade 288 (coefficient of inbreeding 37.5 per cent) was a good breeding cow, and her sire, Whipsnade 281 (coefficient of inbreeding 25 per cent), was one of the outstanding sires in the breed. Royal Beauty, twice winner of the Supreme Interbreed Championship at the Rare Breeds Show, was sired by Whipsnade 281 and was out of a cow by the same bull. Similarly, Dynevor Tawe 22 (coefficient of inbreeding 20.41 per cent) was closely linebred to Dynevor Tawe 3, and her calf had the top weaning weight in the herd in 1991. The feral relatives of the White Park cattle in Chillingham Park in Northumberland have probably been a closed herd for more than 700 years and yet they remain a viable breeding unit, albeit the animals are of much reduced size. Increased inbreeding theoretically leads to increased homozygosity, but in practice heterozygous animals may be more viable and vigorous with a greater chance to beget more progeny.

In other cases a recessive flaw, exposed by inbreeding, can be fatal in a numerically small breed with few bloodlines. Norfolk Horn sheep, already reduced to a single small unit, were found to carry the gene for monorchidism, and there were no clean bloodlines to turn to. The moral must be to apply inbreeding techniques, if necessary, while a breed is sufficiently strong and numerous to overcome any problems that might arise. D. Low observed in 1842: 'A certain feeling of regret may perhaps exist that a race such as the Norfolk Horn, possessing many good properties, should have

*The Durham Ox, a Shorthorn bullock by the same sire as Comet, born in 1796 and painted in 1804; it weighed 1456 kg at 5 years of age and stood 165 cm high at the withers, from a painting by George Garrard, A.R.A.*

been extinguished rather than improved.' In the event he was mistaken: the Norfolk Horn is still hanging on, though by the slenderest of threads.

The effect of developing a breed from a small number of foundation animals is to limit its genetic variability. This applies automatically to all rare breeds, but it applies also to more popular breeds such as the Hereford and the Shorthorn, in which the uniformity of the blood types reflects the degree of the inbreeding bottleneck and distorts any attempt to establish their origin or their relationship to other breeds.

The Thoroughbred horse is international, yet it can trace back its ancestry to a very small number of foundation stallions and mares. It has been fully recorded for pedigree and performance for more than 200 years, and it has developed through phases of linebreeding to an outstanding stallion (Eclipse, St Simon and, currently, Northern Dancer), followed in each case by a period of consolidation. However, it would seem that a plateau of performance may have been reached: there has been no improvement in the ten-year average winning times for the Derby, Oaks and St Leger since 1910, although the improvement from 1850 to 1910 was about ten per cent. This may well be an effect of inbreeding and the limitation of genetic variability, or it may be that the influence of Northern Dancer will provide the impetus for another period of improving performances. Inbreeding in the thoroughbred has proved successful on occasions: Coronation V, a bay filly from France which won the Prix de l'Arc de Triomphe, had a coefficient of inbreeding of 13.28 per cent, plus the basic level of non-current inbreeding (about 8 per cent) that is common throughout the breed. Her great grandsire was Ksar, winner of the French Derby, the St Leger and, on two occasions, the Prix de l'Arc de Triomphe, and he was inbred 6.25 per cent in recent generations.

The extent of inbreeding in the Thoroughbred illustrates the importance of observing certain basic principles. Random or unplanned inbreeding can be detrimental, exposing faults such as weak legs or a nervous temperament. Selective linebreeding to proven individuals concentrates the qualities that are desired. The Clydesdale heavy horse confirms this point. All modern animals trace to Dunure Footprint (1908–30), and the inbreeding from this time probably has enhanced the fashion points of the breed, but it has had an adverse effect on the temperament and intelligence of modern animals compared with those in the early twentieth century. We have been conditioned by moral attitudes to reject incestuous breeding methods, but the danger that we should be more concerned to avoid is the increase in homozygosity, which reduces genetic variability and so leads

*White Park bull, Whipsnade 281, who was the result of a father-daughter mating, and who was also used successfully on his dam and daughters*

to genetic wastage. It is essential to maintain each breed in sufficient numbers to minimise the risk of genetic wastage and genetic drift, and analyses of effective population size and unequal founder effect are more relevant than the use of measures of inbreeding. The fundamental purpose of genetic conservation programmes is to retain the maximum amount of genetic material from founder populations. This is best achieved by calculating the effective founder number for each animal from its pedigree, and retaining those with the highest rating.

This can be illustrated by a comparison of two White Park bulls of very similar breeding, Dynevor Columbus and Ash Lucien. The White Park breed is descended from 75 founder animals but only 15 of these provide approximately 90 per cent of the ancestral contribution. Twelve founder animals are represented in the pedigree of Columbus, and eleven in the pedigree of Lucien, and in both cases the same four founder animals provide about 68 per cent of the ancestral contribution. This similarity is not shown by the coefficient of inbreeding which is markedly different, but it is illustrated very well by the Index based on the effective founder number which was proposed by the author at the Rare Breeds International Congress at Budapest in 1991.

| Bulls | Coefficient of inbreeding | Index (after Alderson) |
|---|---|---|
| Dynevor Columbus | 23.32 | 6.65 |
| Ash Lucien | 10.16 | 5.77 |

From the point of view of genetic conservation, it is desirable to have as many founder animals as possible represented in a pedigree, and to reduce as far as possible the unequal founder effect.

The targets set by the Rare Breeds Survival Trust for the number of bulls to be included in the Semen Bank should be adequate safeguards against the dangers of increasing homozygosity, but those targets are not always met. It can be calculated that if a breed with, say, 100 cows in each

*The last pure-bred Norfolk Horn ram at the National Agricultural Centre before he was accidentally drowned in 1973*

generation was able to call on the services of ten bulls in each generation, the coefficient of inbreeding might be expected to increase by only 1.5 per cent per generation.

In theory, therefore, decisions are taken on the basis of population analyses, but practical limits are imposed by the availability of resources, and each method of genetic conservation must be evaluated not only on its theoretical efficiency but also on its cost–benefit ranking. Ideally, live populations of each breed should be maintained, and supported by Banks of semen and embryos in long-term storage. The live populations should follow the system of rotational mating designed by the author, based on a combination of linebreeding and cyclic crossing. It has been used very successfully with breeds such as the Caspian horse, Norfolk Horn sheep and Portland sheep. For example, in the Portland breed in 1988, fifteen years after the *Combined Flock Book* programme was established, almost half of the foundation ewes and about two-thirds of the foundation rams were represented in the current crop of lambs. Further, as nearly 40 per cent of the registered flocks supply rams, it is clear that a hierarchical structure has not developed.

## Gene Banks and Gene Pools

Two contrasting methods of conserving genetic material have been proposed, and both have their supporters. We have already taken a preliminary look at one system, the gene bank, in considering the storage of semen and embryos and the maintenance of pure-bred live populations. The alternative is the gene pool, a melting pot of mongrelised stock into which the minor breeds would be poured, their genes unrecognisable and inextricably mixed. However indiscriminate and disorderly such a method may seem, it is supported by several eminent geneticists, who are attracted by the prospect of controlling the whole range of genetic variation in a single reservoir of genetic potential. But the concept suffers from two overriding weaknesses in addition to the loss of enthusiastic breeders whose interest lies in pure breeds. In the first instance, the population would need to be

divided into a series of sub-groups, each kept in a different environment, in order to prevent it adjusting to a particular regime, and it would need to be subject to a random-breeding system. A programme of this kind would demand enormous financial resources and it is difficult to imagine any government funding such a vast and cumbersome venture.

The second problem concerns the difficulty of identifying, isolating and utilising a particular characteristic in a 'gene pool' population. It is difficult to comprehend the cost and complexity of providing special conditions designed to spotlight a specific quality which may occur in a small proportion of animals in the population, and which will be associated with other characteristics that differ from animal to animal. I believe that the gene pool concept is unlikely to gain significant acceptance at practical, scientific or governmental levels but the argument continues, and a Canadian geneticist takes the opposite view:

> In a small population the chance of genetic loss from random drift is much increased, and I believe that the most efficient method of conservation is the gene pool. The majority of bovine genes are common to all breeds, and even if selection pressures are applied in one direction within a gene pool by climate, management, fashion or chance, it will be a slow process of change.

It is true that the risk of losses through random genetic drift increases as the size of a population decreases, since even a slight alteration in the number of animals carrying a gene might cause a disproportionate change in the incidence of the gene in the next generation. This is the greatest danger of the gene bank in its application to numerically small breeds. The White Park is such a breed, and Whipsnade 201, a bull born in 1957, has contributed 20.4 per cent of the genes of the breed. Thirty-five years after his birth he continues to be the dominant influence in the breed. The White Park breed might have been significantly different today if another bull of the same generation, the Chester bull, had been selected as the senior sire at Whipsnade instead of Whipsnade 201. The hypothesis is impossible to test, but it is clear that the concentration of genes inherited from Whipsnade 201 may well have resulted in the exclusion of some other qualities, and the cause of genetic conservation would have been served better if the herd had been shared by Whipsnade 201 and any other unrelated bull.

If we accept the superiority of the gene bank as a tool of genetic conservation, it must be with

*The Oxford Sandy and Black pig is no longer included in the lists of the Rare Breeds Survival Trust. Detailed researches have indicated that the modern pigs which bear this name have been derived largely from other breeds, such as the Tamworth, Berkshire, Poland China and Gloucester Old Spots*

*Reconstructed Aurochs. The programme of reconstruction was based on visual characteristics, and we cannot be sure that it resembles the Aurochs in any more than a very superficial manner*

the proviso that the widest possible range of unrelated males is used within each minority breed. There must be a readily available source of fully identified semen, documented as far as possible with the characteristics and qualities of the donor bull. This is the purpose of the Semen Bank established by the Rare Breeds Survival Trust and the Milk Marketing Board. Plant breeders have much to teach us in this matter. The value of introducing 'wild genes' into the domestic stocks of both potato and oat crops has been mentioned earlier with particular reference to disease resistance. In both cases it was considered more efficient to maintain a gene bank. The same principles apply to livestock, although in a less straightforward manner. Resistance to Marek's disease is well documented in some strains of poultry. Soay sheep are resistant to footrot, and among sheep in general certain haemoglobin factors are associated with increased viability. If disease resistance is accepted as an inherited factor, it could be much more easily introduced by direct access to, say, Soay rams, rather than the long and uncertain process of extracting it from a gene pool.

It is very easy to ignore the human element. Abstract arguments on the relative merits of gene banks and gene pools are irrelevant unless the people involved are able and willing to understand the concepts and principles of genetic conservation. If scientists regard rare breeds as 'the waste products of the process of domestication' and commercial breeders arbitrarily class them as by-gones in farm park collections, or if conservationists raise them on academic pedestals, then the whole argument becomes sterile. Such extreme postures are likely to be counter-productive, and most of the successes in genetic conservation in various parts of the world have been achieved by conservationists, breeders and scientists working together.

## Conservation

Between the two World Wars, the brothers Heck carried out well-publicised experiments in Germany to reconstruct the Aurochs. Each worked to his own formula, but both breeding programmes were based on the principle of crossing selected modern breeds of cattle in order that genes handed down from their wild ancestors might be recombined to produce living Aurochsen. Heinz Heck, Director of the Tierpark Hellabrun in Munich, used Podolian steppe cattle, Highlands, Alpine cattle from Algau and Werdenfels, Friesians and Corsicans, while his brother Lutz, Director of the Berlin Zoological Gardens, used Spanish and Camargue fighting bulls, White Parks and Corsicans. The cattle in the two groups were said to be indistinguishable, but probably all that the brothers succeeded in doing was to create an animal, based heavily on Corsican cattle, which bore a superficial resemblance to a distant and imprecisely documented ancestor. No one can claim more with con-

*The Blue Albion is believed to be extinct. Present-day blue cattle probably are the result of crosses between Friesian and Shorthorn cattle*

viction, and we know nothing of the animals' physiological characteristics or productive standards. Apart from the enormous publicity which the experiments received, and the value of observing behavioural regression when domestic stock becomes feral, the only importance of the bred-back Aurochs has been to demonstrate quite clearly that we must accept breeds as they are now, and not devalue our efforts by attempting to legitimise the reconstruction of original types that were often not even clearly defined.

Even with more recent cases of extinction there can be no justification for attempts to recreate breeds of domestic livestock. The Chantecler breed of chicken was established c.1918 at Oka Monastery in Quebec. It was a big, meaty, white, dual-purpose breed with a walnut comb. It is extinct, but a phenotypically correct type has been reconstructed by exhibition breeders. Both the Suffolk Dun and the Irish Dun were valuable breeds of dairy cattle in the British Isles that became extinct in the present century. Both could have contributed to the efficiency of the dairy industry today. We know a good deal about them – their appearance, their production, their ancestry and their descendants – but it is wishful thinking to believe that they could be reconstructed by the judicious blending of extant related breeds. Attempts have been made to re-create the Blue Albion breed of cattle and the Oxford Sandy and Black breed of pig. The Blue Albion Breed Society is of relatively recent origin, having been formed in 1921. The last Herd Book was published in 1937, the last AGM was held in 1940, the Society was dissolved in 1966, and the last bull was licensed in 1972. A direct relationship cannot be demonstrated between animals currently known as Blue Albion and those registered with the Breed Society; blood-typing of animals in 1980 showed an affinity to Friesian cattle. The Oxford Sandy and Black probably had ceased to exist before 1970, and a mixture of breeds have been crossed to combine the supposed visual characteristics of the extinct breed. Animals which now masquerade under the names of the Chantecler, Blue Albion and the Oxford Sandy and Black are derived from other breeds, and are not accepted as legitimate breeds. Their irrevocable loss must be regretted, but nevertheless accepted.

When a breed has survived, albeit as a type only vaguely reminiscent of its earlier representatives, the same principles should apply. It must be accepted on its present attributes, clearly distinguishing between the modification of a breed and the re-creation of a breed. Early Gloucester cattle were developed as a dairy breed two centuries ago, when their milk was processed into Double Gloucester cheese. Throughout their recorded history they have been under pressure from

*Gloucester cow in 1939, showing the typical lineback pattern and white tail. Some animals also have a white 'garter' around the hind legs just above the hocks*

currently popular breeds – the Longhorn, followed by the Shorthorn and, finally, the Friesian. The Gloucester has outlived these threats but has not managed to escape progressive dilution of its ancestral genotype with considerable quantities of Shorthorn and Friesian blood. It remains a recognisable entity by virtue of its colour pattern, white finching and a white tail. These are hallmarks of the breed that have survived each phase of crossbreeding with a persistence that doubtless will ensure the continuing existence of the Gloucester as a visually distinctive type.

The Bathurst and Wickcourt herds have exerted a major influence on the breed since the Second World War. The Bathurst herd was dispersed in 1966, and the Wickcourt in 1972; each fragment of these herds became the nucleus of a new breeding unit, thus generating the fresh enthusiasm that led to the formation of a Breed Society in 1973. Would that it had been so straightforward. Lord Bathurst was a man of enquiring mind and experimented extensively with his Gloucester cattle. He recorded his thoughts in an article for *The Field* in 1930:

> It was not until 1922 that I first bought a few Gloucester heifers and a bull to found my herd, adding to it during the next two years when any cattle came into the market. I did not have much luck to start with, as a large proportion of the calves were bull calves; then there was difficulty in getting the cows in calf, many of them turning several times. I found that this did not happen in the case of Shorthorn heifers covered by the Gloucester bull, and I had an idea that it would be a good thing to introduce some outside blood, as for many years the pure-bred Gloucesters must have been terribly inbred. [Author's note: I have found the same effect among present-day Gloucesters. The conception rates are good when using Gloucester semen for crossbreeding, but very poor when used for pure-breeding.]
>
> It was a well-known fact that farmers in the Beaufort or Berkeley countries constantly used Gloucester bulls, as they particularly liked the first cross heifers which they found to be their best milkers. Why not, therefore, go on with this and grade up a new and refreshed strain of Gloucester cattle, retaining the old characteristics which so improved as to fully recorded milk production that they would become a popular and desirable breed for many cattle breeders to possess.
>
> The interest of this seemed enormous, much more so than going into the market and buying already made 1000-gallon Shorthorn cows at large prices, and trying to breed other 1000-gallon heifers. So for the last few years I have been quietly working to grade up Gloucester cattle to the coveted 1000-gallon cow.
>
> The difficulty at starting was that there were no milk records to go by when purchasing a bull, a factor that even now with the knowledge of the dam's record does not always ensure an improvement in the record of the heifer. With patience and a few more years of experience that may become an easier matter. Meanwhile the interest increases every year as the home-bred heifers come into milk.

Last year I began a new experiment for the introduction of new blood, and my reason for taking this course is as follows. The Gloucester cattle are supposed to have been brought to Badminton by a Duke of Beaufort from Wales about 150 years ago. The marking and colour of Gloucester cattle are much like the old Glamorgan breed now practically extinct. May it not, therefore, be conjectured that the cattle now called Gloucester are really a slightly varied offshoot of the Glamorgan breed, who are in turn a variant descended from the old Black Welsh cattle?

The ancient breed of Welsh cattle was black, but very small, and I believe that in order to increase their size some bulls of large white wild cattle, like the Chillingham, now called Park Cattle, were used. Any of the calves that came white were ruthlessly destroyed, so as to preserve the Welsh black characteristic; but for many years after there appeared occasionally a white calf with black points.

I was told that the late Lord Dynevor kept some of these White-Park-marked calves and established a herd which is still growing and going strong. Last year I asked the present Lord Dynevor if he could let me have a white bull of this breed, and this he very kindly did.

In addition to the introduction of Shorthorn, Welsh Black and White Park cattle documented here, Friesians completed the pattern at a later date. Consequently, when the herd was dispersed a generation later, one of Lord Bathurst's sons, the Hon. W. R. S. Bathurst, wrote, 'My late brother's herd includes a good many beasts that look like Gloucesters, but I doubt if any are of pure descent.'

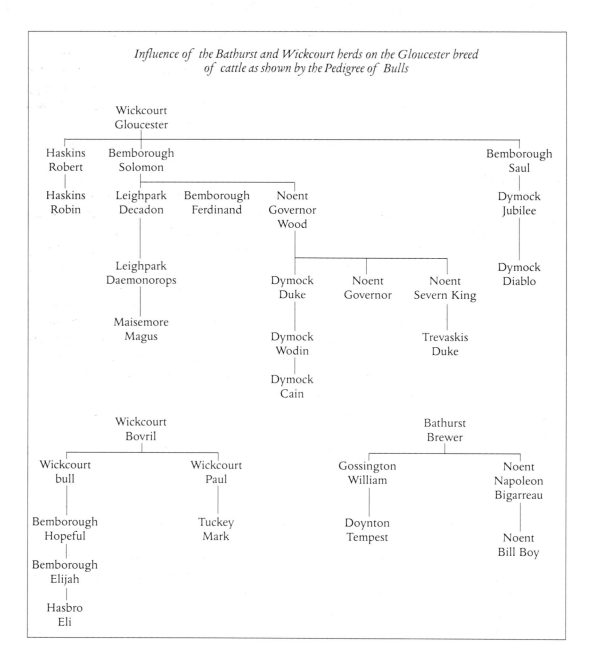

*Influence of the Bathurst and Wickcourt herds on the Gloucester breed of cattle as shown by the Pedigree of Bulls*

*A British White herd in South Australia. The original cows were imported by A. Hordern in 1958 and were in-calf to a Galloway bull. Shorthorn crosses were introduced at a later stage, and thus these cattle are not pure*

Similarly it is reported that fertility problems in the Wickcourt herd had been solved by using a Jersey bull, so that when the newly-formed Breed Society set up a Herd Book it could do little other than accept animals which were correctly marked, ignoring to a large extent tacitly admitted impurities. There were only two choices. Either the 'breed' could be accepted as it was in 1973, adulteration and all, or it could be rejected completely as a colourmarked product of planned mongrelisation. There was no way of compromise, and there was little doubt about acceptance – the upsurge of regional fervour in Britain and the growing popularity of amenity centres ensured that – but it was a new Gloucester, with milky strains based on the Bathurst concoction, and beefier characteristics introduced through Wickcourt Gloucester. The present-day animals may bear limited resemblances to the cattle whose milk laid the foundation of the Double Gloucester cheese industry two centuries ago, or even to the angular dairy-like cows that dominated the show classes in the 1930s, but they represent the genetic material available, and it is with them that we must work.

The history of British White cattle is comparable in many ways to that of the Gloucester. During its history, the breed has been influenced by several other breeds and has changed its type as a result. White, polled cattle emerged from obscure beginnings into the clear light of documented development at Whalley Abbey in Lancashire. When that herd was disbanded in 1697, they spread to Gisburne Park in Yorkshire, Middleton Park near Manchester and, probably, to Somerford in Cheshire. These herds became the mainspring for expansion of the breed, although the greatest concentration of British White cattle has been found, for the last 100 years at least, in East Anglia. Throughout the breed's development its type has been changing constantly. There is no certainty about its origins, but the likelihood is that a polled Scandinavian bull from the East coast of England was crossed with white cattle from the Trough of Bowland to produce a polled, colour-marked breed.

Initially the British White was developed as a dual-purpose breed with a tendency to dairy type. Some very respectable milk yields were achieved. In 1928 the Bolwick herd averaged 4923 kg milk per cow, and in the 1940s Bawdeswell Catmint gave almost 16,350 kg milk in three years. By the mid-1970s the Hevingham herd, an offshoot of the Bolwick herd and the last milk-recorded herd, averaged only 3273 kg per cow and 2764 kg per heifer per lactation, when the national average for dairy cows in Great Britain was 4668 kg per lactation.

Today, a casual observer of the British White breed would be forgiven for disputing its classification as a dual-purpose/dairy breed, and even a cursory glance through the archives will reveal the reason. Records in the half century between 1925 and 1975 are littered with introductions of alien blood. Apart from minor flirtations with Guernsey crosses, the breed has been influenced mainly by three others, the Shorthorn, the Fjallras from Sweden, and finally, in the 1960s and 1970s, the

White Galloway. The only reasonably constant factor in this process has been colour, and its distinctive pattern is the one characteristic which the British White has retained through fluctuating fortunes and a shifting geographical distribution. The beefy, single-suckle type that has come to the fore in the 1970s is not comparable to the dairy animals of earlier years. The beefy Galloway influence has not permeated the entire breed, but in North America (where it is confusingly called the White Park) and Australia the breed is much less pure. It may still be possible in Britain to direct the main emphasis of conservation towards those animals and herds which have suffered least from crossing with other breeds.

This is realistic conservation. It is very easy to get carried away on the magic carpet of retrospective idealism, and equally easy on the other hand to be trampled underfoot in the commercial crush, but imaginative conservation requires both the ability to accept that what is already done is part of the past, and a genuine desire to protect the wealth of genetic material that still remains.

## Breed Priorities

It has been assumed that both Gloucester and British White cattle should be saved from extinction, despite their blemished records, but on what basis was that decision taken? Was it the right decision? Clearly defined criteria must be applied, not only to determine which breeds qualify for support, but also to establish an order of priorities among the breeds which have a claim on the resources which are available for their preservation.

The Rare Breeds Survival Trust uses an Acceptance Procedure which I devised in 1975. It is, at base, a preliminary screening process to assess the eligibility of each breed, followed by the use of numerical status to establish priorities. The critical population size is measured in the number of females used for pure-breeding, and is calculated from a formula based on three factors: the ratio of breeding males to breeding females, the longevity of the breeding females, and the reproductive rate.

Details of the Acceptance Procedure are as follows:

*Rare Breeds Acceptance Procedure*

---

### Section A

1 Has there been an accepted Stud/Herd/Flock Book for at least six generations?
2 Have other breeds contributed less than 20 per cent of the genotype of the breed in the last six generations?
3 Are the parent breeds used in the formation of this breed no longer available?
4 Has it existed continuously for 75 years?

*If the answer to 4 is the affirmative, and if two or three of the other answers are affirmitive, proceed to Section B*

### Section B

1 To be included in the lists there should be less than the following number of breeding females in the breed:

| Cattle 750 | Goats 500 | Horses 1000 |
|---|---|---|
| Pigs 500 | Sheep 1500 | |

2 Breeds with four or less distinct male lines may be included. A distinct male line has no ancestors in common with other lines up to and including the great-grandparent generation.
*Proceed to Section C.*

### Section C

1 Are the numbers of the breed decreasing significantly?
2 Is the breed found in less than four significant units which are more than 50 miles apart?

*Affirmative answers to these questions give the breed a higher priority.*

---

*Irish Moiled cow. This breed has benefited from the interest of Dr Ian Gill at Liverpool University. He has formulated and implemented a co-ordinated breeding programme*

An alternative procedure is illustrated below. The criteria used are very similar to those in the Trust's method, but the priorities are expressed as a score rather than a category. The measure of Genetic Value takes into account antiquity, purity, distinctiveness and, to a lesser degree, historical importance and current commercial qualities. Vulnerability is assessed from the statistics of effective population size, population trends and location.

Among the British breeds of cattle which are classed as vulnerable the Kerry, the Irish Moiled and the Dexter originated in Ireland, and these three breeds illustrate very well the index method of ranking rare breeds.

*Endangered Breeds of British Cattle*

| Breed | Genetic Value (a) | Vunerability (b) | Priority Rating $\sqrt{a^2 + b^2}$ | Current Category |
|---|---|---|---|---|
| White Park | 84.5 | 88.3 | 122.22 | Endangered |
| Kerry | 81.0 | 89.6 | 120.79 | Critical |
| Shetland | 76.0 | 91.5 | 118.95 | Critical |
| Vaynol | 53.0 | 97.6 | 111.06 | Critical |
| Irish Moiled | 52.5 | 92.9 | 106.71 | Critical |
| Red Polled | 71.0 | 66.1 | 97.01 | Vulnerable |
| Beef Shorthorn | 59.0 | 74.9 | 95.35 | Vulnerable |
| Gloucester | 41.5 | 79.2 | 89.41 | Vulnerable |
| Belted Galloway | 49.0 | 72.9 | 87.84 | Minority |
| Longhorn | 72.0 | 47.3 | 86.15 | Minority |
| Dexter | 62.0 | 53.2 | 81.70 | Minority |
| British White | 53.0 | 60.3 | 80.28 | At Risk |
| Devon | 64.0 | 13.5 | 65.41 | Watching |
| Lincoln Red | 63.0 | 6.4 | 63.32 | Watching |

The Kerry is one of the purest surviving descendants of cattle brought to Britain in the early part of the second millennium BC. Having remained very largely free of influence from other breeds, it possesses a distinctive type that separates it even from related breeds such as the Welsh Black. The Kerry's alert, graceful quality, accentuated by the light head and upturned, black-tipped horns, makes it a very appealing breed. Nevertheless it is in danger. There are fewer than 400

*A dwarf Dexter cow, Woodmagic Mallemuck, bred by Mrs B. Rutherford in Devon*

breeding cows, and in recent years important herds have been dispersed. At the same time, renewed interest among breeders in the United Kingdom saves the outlook from being entirely gloomy. The breed's high rating for genetic value, combined with its vulnerable numerical status, makes it a breed of high priority.

Neither the Dexter nor the Irish Moiled can claim the same degree of genetic importance, but the Irish Moiled ranks alongside the Kerry in priority because it is particularly vulnerable, with less than 100 breeding cows. The breed has recovered from the brink of extinction in recent years, with increased interest from breeders in Ulster and England, and a breeding programme has been devised by Dr Ian Gill of Liverpool University. The origin of the Irish Moiled can be attributed to the Vikings, who made Ireland one of their major centres. Since the Second World War Shorthorn and Lincoln Red blood has been introduced, and a polled Finnish bull was imported in 1950. While the Irish Moiled is indubitably a breed, these alien crosses lower its genetic value.

The Dexter has been affected in the same way. In the 1930s various attempts to decrease the incidence of 'bulldog' calves led to the surreptitious inclusion of Welsh Black, Aberdeen Angus and Jersey cattle. Again, more recently, the experimental bulls Atlantic Finbar and Statenboro Fircone, both containing Jersey and Aberdeen Angus blood, were used, and there is also an official grading-up procedure. In addition, the breed's increasing popularity, partly stimulated by their value as house-cows and on smallholdings, might suggest that it should not be included in the priority lists. It is, however, a true miniature breed – or dwarf, depending on your viewpoint. This is such a distinctive characteristic that it should be conserved, and it is sufficiently significant to keep the Dexter in the survival priority ratings, albeit in a relatively modest position.

Other species can be evaluated in the same way, and it is particularly important to have a standard yardstick such as this for species with a shorter generation interval, where new breeds and varieties can be created very quickly. Poultry provide an extreme example, where a new breed can be created and established within a few years, and a new variety is achieved by a simple change of colour. The process with pigs and sheep is less rapid, but even so new breeds have emerged since the Second World War. The Salz sheep, developed by Prof Isidro Sierra in Spain, the Camborough pig and Colbred sheep are prime examples, and Oscar Colburn (creator of the Colbred) estimated that the whole process of the creation of a new breed of sheep could be completed in twenty years.

Although the Colbred and the Camborough are classed officially as breeds, they are more comparable to modern hybrids and, as such, could not be considered as distinct types even if they were in danger of dying out. They have not existed long enough to earn a place in the gallery of

*Northern Dairy Shorthorn bull, Winbrook Atom 2nd, from the sire line of Prince (396, born 1942), at the Great Yorkshire Show in 1974. He is of the favoured light-roan colour, and has been dehorned; his semen has been stored in the Semen Bank*

British breeds, and as their parent breeds are extant they could be re-created at any time should the need arise. The Acceptance Procedure places a minimum period of continuous existence for a breed of seventy-five years before it qualifies for inclusion. A breed such as the Castlemilk Moorit, evolved by the Buchanan-Jardine family on their estate in Scotland early this century, has only recently reached the required seniority for acceptance.

Distinctness of type is an important factor, but it is more difficult to define. It is complicated by the effects of convergent and divergent evolution, which may mask the true original type. The Shorthorn family is an excellent example. All the breeds in this group are offshoots of the old Durham or Teeswater cattle, but the Northern Dairy Shorthorn at one extreme has little in common with the Beef Shorthorn at the other. The squat, heavily-fleshed Beef Shorthorn is very much akin to the Aberdeen Angus, although it is now being increased in size by crossing with the Maine-Anjou. The Northern Dairy Shorthorn is an alert, active hill breed that compares more closely with a hardy Ayrshire or a robust Kerry. Its stylish quality betrays little of its common ancestry 200 years ago with either the Beef Shorthorn or the Dairy Shorthorn. Its distinctiveness should assure the breed of a high priority in the grand strategy of genetic conservation.

However, it is possible that the Northern Dairy Shorthorn has been lost to future generations, that it will disappear in the ancient archives of Coates Herd Book, and that it will be absorbed into the Dairy Shorthorn breed. The blame may be laid at the door of apathetic breeders or of ill-formed scientific dogma, but excuses will not revive an extinct breed. The way ahead for the Northern Dairy Shorthorn and other minority breeds is ill-defined, beset with contradictions, and full of pitfalls. The saving of an endangered breed demands a scientific approach, yet it must not offend idealistic emotions. It requires discipline, but must not stifle enthusiasm; it must pay due regard to biological efficiency rather than fashion, demonstrate and encourage the commercial

value of these breeds without attracting speculative interests, and ensure purity of descent without reducing genetic variability. Those dedicated to the conservation of endangered breeds must possess tolerance and a realisation that time will not stand still, so that idealism must be tempered with realism. Big demands – some would say unreasonable – and yet the events of the last two decades give much cause for optimism. We can cite the Jacob sheep as an example of a breed that was almost unknown in the 1960s, but is now a viable and vigorous part of the British sheep industry. We can show that, whereas the Charolais was a rare breed 150 years ago, it is now a beef breed of international importance. Just as the Charolais was conserved then, we should now conserve even those breeds which have no apparent relevance.

*Beef Shorthorn bull. In common with other native British beef breeds, the Beef Shorthorn has declined in competition with imported breeds in the last two decades*

## Rare Breeds Survival Trust

The development of the Rare Breeds Survival Trust has matched closely the progress of genetic conservation in Great Britain, and it has evolved an effective and comprehensive policy which could well be used as a model for other organisations. Initially the Trust was concerned primarily to meet urgent problems facing endangered breeds. Thus the island of Linga Holm was purchased as a safe haven for a flock of North Ronaldsay sheep, and boars of the Tamworth and Berkshire breeds were imported from Australia to resuscitate the bloodlines in Britain. Thereafter a planned ongoing policy was implemented.

The basic need in a policy of genetic conservation is to identify the existing populations, and this has been achieved by a regular survey of numbers of both breeding stock and breeding units within each breed. Conservation is thus effected through the medium of recognised breeds, which are identified by means of the Acceptance Procedure. Thereafter it is necessary to record the ancestry of each animal, as is done for sheep in the *Combined Flock Book,* and for pigs through a scheme operated in conjunction with the British Pig Association. Pedigree records enable relationships and founder effects to be calculated, and the Trust has established a Breed Structure Analysis project based on its in-house computer, and has supported studies on blood-typing and genetic distancing.

Genetic material is conserved both in live populations and in banks of frozen semen and embryos. The ownership of live populations is undertaken if necessary, as with North Ronaldsay sheep and Bagot goats, but more usually support is provided through financial incentives paid to breeders. For example, financial incentives first paid in respect of Middle White boars in 1980 now encourage breeders of all rare breeds of pig to keep animals for pure-breeding, and the Trust has co-operated with the Shetland Islands Council to provide similar incentives for Shetland cattle. Semen is stored from a representative sample of bulls within an ongoing programme, and this programme is being extended to include pigs, sheep and goats. Embryos will eventually be collected from a representative sample of females in each breed, at intervals of five generations. Owners of rare breeds are encouraged to form breeders' groups where no Breed Society exists, and to help to monitor endangered lines within each breed. Group breeding schemes are prepared to counteract any shift towards a hierarchical breed structure. Each breed is evaluated, not only to assess its potential value within commercial systems, but also to research any problems which are identified. Thus most rare breeds of pig have been shown to produce high-quality meat, primitive breeds of sheep compare favourably with popular breeds as dams of lambs for slaughter, and some rare breeds of cattle experience fewer problems at parturition. Research is initiated into problems, and a confidential register of congenital defects is maintained.

Finally, the Trust promotes rare breeds to reach a wider audience, not only to encourage more breeders to establish breeding units, but also to obtain funds for its programmes. The Trust is an independent organisation and thus can not command automatic support from state agencies. A monthly magazine, *The Ark,* is the main method of publicising rare breeds, but the Trust organises several important events. The annual Show and Sale is the major event, demonstrations are mounted at many of the larger agricultural shows, and workshops, seminars and conferences are held as necessary. Wool producers have been assisted by negotiating the exemption of several rare breeds from the British Wool Marketing Board monopoly of wool marketing, and specialist outlets for meat have been developed, both with private breeders, such as Mrs Anne Petch for speciality traditional meats, and with other trade outlets.

The success of these evaluation, education, research and promotion programmes gives greater security to rare breeds in the future, and justifies the conservation programme. The importance of the Trust's programme can be measured by the increase in the numbers of almost all the rare breeds in Britain since the Trust was established in 1973. For example, Shropshire sheep increased from 431 ewes in 1974 to 1871 ewes in 1992, Portland sheep from 85 to 744 ewes, White Park cattle from 65 to 248 cows, and Longhorn cattle from 120 to 1050 cows in the same period. These breeds, and others, have accepted the chance to survive and to play their part in the future.

# APPENDIX I

# Colour Inheritance

### Colour Inheritance in Sheep

Coat colour in sheep is controlled primarily by a multiple series of alleles at the locus 'A'. The dominant gene is $A^{wh}$ for white. Below in turn come $A^g$ (and others) for grey, $A^w$ for the moufflon pattern, and finally the recessive gene a, which must be present in the homozygous state to permit the expression of whole-colour at locus 'B'. Thus the locus 'A' exerts an epistatic effect on locus 'B'. Black and brown are the two colours which occur at this locus, and the gene B for black is dominant to the gene b for brown.

Thus the main genotypes are as follows:

| | | | | |
|---|---|---|---|---|
| White | $A^{wh}A^{wh}BB$ | $A^{wh}A^gBB$ | $A^{wh}A^wBB$ | $A^{wh}aBB$ |
| | $A^{wh}A^{wh}Bd$ | $A^{wh}A^gBb$ | $A^{wh}A^wBb$ | $A^{wh}aBb$ |
| | $A^{wh}A^{wh}bb$ | $A^{wh}A^gbb$ | $A^{wh}A^wbb$ | $A^{wh}abb$ |
| Grey | $A^gA^gBB$ | $A^gA^wBB$ | $A^gaBB$ | |
| | $A^gA^gBb$ | $A^gA^wBb$ | $A^gaBb$ | |
| Grey-brown | $A^gA^gbb$ | $A^gA^wbb$ | $A^gabb$ | |
| Soay pattern dark colour | $A^wA^wBB$ | $A^waBB$ | | |
| | $A^wA^wBb$ | $A^waBb$ | | |
| Soay pattern light colour | $A^wA^wbb$ | $A^wabb$ | | |
| Black | aaBB | | | |
| | aaBb | | | |
| Brown | aabb | | | |

Genes at two other loci, 'E' and 'S', also effect colour in British sheep.
'E' produces dominant black, and 'S' produces a spotted fleece.

### Colour Inheritance in Horses

Coat colour in horses is determined basically by the interaction of genes at the 'A' and 'B' loci. The dominant allele at the 'A' locus produces the drab colour of wild horses, as seen in Przewalski's horse, necessary for camouflage. It is not present in domestic horses as it has mutated to other alleles which give brighter colours favoured in domestication. The dominant B allele at the 'B' locus produces black, and the recessive b allele produces liver (chocolate). These are modified by the A and $a^t$ alleles to bay and brown, but are not affected by the a allele.

The dominant $E^D$ allele at the 'E' locus does not affect the basic black or liver colour. The E allele produces fading colour, while the recessive e allele produces chestnut.

The 'C' and 'D' loci are responsible for colour dilution. The dominant C allele causes no dilution, but $c^{cr}$ dilutes red pigment, changing chestnut progressively to palomino and cremello, and bay to dun. The dominant D allele dilutes chestnut to yellow dun, and black to grulla, but the recessive d allele has no effect.

Among the various colours of horses, chestnut and cremello, for example, always breed true, while colours such as palomino, dun, buckskin, roan and dominant white do not breed true. Roan and dominant white are controlled by genes which are lethal when homozygous.

The colour of spotted horses is controlled by a series of genes, so that there are many different types and degrees of spotting.

Grey is caused by the dominant G allele at the 'G' locus, and is dominant to other colours. Foals which carry the G allele are born with the colour determined by the rest of their genotype, but the greying increases with age and eventually the animal will appear white. Thus an animal with the genotype A–B– (bay colour) CCdd (no dilution) E– (not chestnut) G– (grey) would be born bay and turn grey.

The genotype of animals of unusual colour can be mapped out by an analysis of their own colour and that of their ancestors and progeny. Shirine, a Caspian mare rescued from Iran, is a light red dun with a dorsal stripe ($a^t$–bb $Cc^{cr}$ D–ee gg). $a^t$ determines the dorsal stripe, bb and ee that the basic colour is chestnut with no black, $Cc^{cr}$ and D– that the colour is doubly diluted, and gg that grey is not present. She does not breed true for colour, because she is heterozygous at the 'C' locus in the same way as a palomino.

# APPENDIX II

# Rare Breeds Survival Trust

*Advisory Committee (March 1973)*

| | |
|---|---|
| G. L. H. Alderson | Farmer and International Livestock Consultant |
| M. D. M. Ann | Farm Park Proprietor |
| Professor J. C. Bowman | University of Reading |
| J. Cator | Farmer |
| J. Cole-Morgan | Agricultural Research Council |
| R. P. Cooper | Farmer |
| The Earl of Cranbrook | Natural Environment Research Council |
| C. V. T. Dadd | Royal Agricultural Society of England |
| Sir Dudley Forwood, Bt | Royal Agricultural Society of England |
| J. L. Henson | Farmer and Farm Park Proprietor |
| Professor P. A. Jewell | University of London |
| W. Longrigg | Agricultural Development and Advisory Service |
| A. J. Manchester | National Pig Breeders' Association |
| Capt. C. Pitman | Fauna Preservation Society |
| Dr I. W. Rowlands | Zoological Society of London |
| Mrs E. R. Wheatley-Hubbard | Farmer and Royal Agricultural Society of England |

*Officers in 1993*

| | |
|---|---|
| Patron | HRH The Prince of Wales |
| President | Lord Barber of Tewkesbury |
| Chairman | D. W. Reeves |
| Vice-Chairman | G.E. Cloke |
| Executive Director | G. L. H. Alderson |
| Administration Director | R. Terry |
| Chairman of the Breed Liaison Committee | G. E. Cloke |
| Chairman of the Project Development Committee | J. R. Mulholland |
| Chairman of the Show and Sale Committee | A. J. Hawtin |

# BIBLIOGRAPHY

Adalsteinsson, S. 'Colour Inheritance in Icelandic Sheep', *J. Agr. Res. Icel.* II, pp. 3-135 (1970)
 'Genetics of Breeding Coloured Sheep in Iceland and Scandinavia', *Proc. of Breeding Coloured Sheep Congress* (Adelaide, 1979).
Alderson, G. L. H. *The Observer's Book of Farm Animals* (Frederick Warne, London, 1976)
 'Sheep Shearing and Culling on Linga Holm', *The Ark* Vol. IV, No. 9 (1977)
 'Work done on the Conservation of Animal Genetic Resources in the UK' (Paper to the UNEP/FAO Technical Consultation on Animal Genetic Resources Conservation and Management, Rome, 1980)
 'A Breeding Policy for Minority Breeds', *International Caspian Stud Book,* Vol. III (Countrywide Livestock Ltd, 1983)
 *Rare Breeds* (Shire Publications, Aylesbury, 1984)
 'Selection Methods and Breeding Programmes used in the Conservation of Rare Breeds of Coloured Sheep', Paper to the World Congress of Coloured Sheep (New Zealand, 1984)
 'An Analysis of the Breed Structure of the Exmoor Pony', (1985, unpublished)
 'The History, Development and Qualities of White Park Cattle', *The Herd Book of White Park Cattle,* Vol. V (Countrywide Livestock Ltd, 1987)
 'An Analysis of the Sire Lines in the Cleveland Bay Breed of Horse', (1988, unpublished)
 'Genetic Conservation of Domestic Livestock', (ed.) (C.A.B. International, U.K. 1990)
 'Polycerate Inheritance', *The Ark* Vol. XIX, No. 5 (1992)
Alderson, G. L. H. and Bodo, I. (eds.) 'Genetic Conservation of Domestic Livestock', Vol. 2 (C.A.B. International, U.K. 1992)
Alderson, G. L. H. and Hindson, J. C. *Ash Farm Records* (in press)

Barrie, J. 'The Clydesdale Horse' (1903, unpublished)
Bates, C. J. *Thomas Bates and the Kirklevington Shorthorns* (Newcastle-upon-Tyne, 1897)
Blaxter, K. L., *et.al. Farming the Red Deer* (HMSO, Edinburgh, 1974)
Boston, E. *Jersey Cattle* (Faber & Faber, London, 1954)
Burns, M. 'Wensleydale Sheep – The Kemp Killers', *The Ark* Vol. V, No. 2 (1978)

Centre for Agricultural Strategy, *Land for Agriculture* (Reading, 1976)
Chivers, K. *The Shire Horse* (J. A. Allen, London, 1976)
Clark, J. L. *The Great Arc of the Wild Sheep* (University of Oklahoma Press, USA, 1 964)
Clutton-Brock, J. *Domesticated Animals* (Heinemann, London, 1981)
Countrywide Livestock Ltd. 'An Analysis of Thoroughbred Stallions in the USA' (1973, unpublished)

Dent, A. A., & Goodall, D. M. *The Foals of Epona* (Gallery Press, London, 1962)
Dobie, J. F. *The Longhorns* (Nicholson & Watson, London, 1943)

Elwes, H. J. *A Guide to the Primitive Breeds of Sheep and their Crosses* (Edinburgh, 1913)
Epstein, H. *The Origin of the Domestic Animals of Africa* (Leipzig, 1970)

Firouz, L. *The Caspian Miniature Horse of Iran* (Field Research Projects, Miami, USA, 1972)
FAO. *Pilot Study on the Conservation of Animal Genetic Resources* (Rome, 1975)
Fowler, S. H. 'The Texas Longhorn', *The Ark* Vol. I, No. 7 (1974)

French, M. H., *et.al. European Breeds of Cattle* (FAO, Rome, 1966, 2 vols)

Gahne, B., Danell, O., & S Jorgren, T. *Fur Skin Characteristics and Breeding of the Gotland Sheep*
(Report of the 3rd International Symposium on Karakul Sheep Breeding, 1975)
Gates, S. 'The Exmoor Pony in 1977', *The Ark* Vol. IV, No. 6 (1977)
Geist, V. *Mountain Sheep: A Study in Behaviour and Evolution* (University of Chicago Press,
USA, 1971 )
Groves, C. P. *Horses, Asses and Zebras in the Wild* (David & Charles, Newton Abbot, Devon, 1974)

Hammond, A. *World Resources 1992–3,* (Oxford University Press, 1992)
Hindson, J. C. 'Iodine Levels in the Milk of North Ronaldsay Ewes', *The Ark* Vol. III, No. 5
(1976)

Isaac, E. 'The Geography of Domestication' (1970)

Jankovich, M. *They Rode into Europe* (Harrap, London, trans. A. Dent, 1971)
Jewell, P. A., *et.al.* (eds). *Island Survivors: The Ecology of the Soay Sheep of St Kilda* (Athlone Press,
London, 1974)
Jones, C. B. (ed.) *Livestock of the Farm* (Gresham Publishing, London, 1920, 6 vols)

Kaufman, M. H., Huberman, E., & Sachs, L. 'Genetic Control of Haploid Parthenogenetic
Development in Mammalian Embryos', *Nature* 254 (1975)
Kleberg,J.,Jr. *The Santa Gertrudis Breed of Beef Cattle (1954, pamphlet)*

Lasley, J. F. *Genetics of Livestock Improvement* (Prentice Hall, Englewood Cliffs, NJ, USA, 1963)
Lerner, I. M., & Donald, H. P. *Modern Developments in Animal Breeding* (Academic Press, London,
1966)
Low, D. *Domesticated Animals of the British Isles* (Longman Green, London, 1842)
Lush, J. L. *Animal Breeding Plans* (Iowa State University Press, USA, 3rd ed, 1945)

Mason, I. L. *The Classification of West African Livestock* (Commonwealth Agricultural Bureaux,
1951)
*The Sheep Breeds of the Mediterranean* (FAO, Rome, 1967)
*A World Dictionary of Livestock Breeds, Types and Varieties* (Commonwealth Agricultural Bureaux,
3rd ed., 1988)
*Hybridization between Bison and Cattle* (FAO, Rome, 1975)
Maurant, A. E., & Zeuner, F. E. (eds). *Man and Cattle* (Royal Anthropological Institute of GB and
Ireland, 1963)
McClelland, T. H., Bonaiti, B., & Taylor, StC.S. 'Breed Differences in Body Composition of
Equally Mature Sheep', *J. of B.S.A.P.* 23, 3 (1976)

Paterson, I. W. The foraging strategy of the seaweed-eating sheep on North Ronaldsay, Orkney
(PhD thesis, Cambridge, 1984)
Pawson, H.C. *Robert Bakewell* (Crosby Lockwood & Sons, London, 1957)
Payne, J. M. 'Metabolic Profiles', *Vet. Record* 87 (1970)
Pegler, H. S. H. *The Book of the Goat* (6th ed., 1925)
Pitt-Rivers, A. *Excavations in Cranborne Chase 1887-1905*
Portal, M., & Quittet, E. *Les Races Porcines Françaises* (Ministere de l'Agriculture, Paris, 1956)
Porter, V. *Practical Rare Breeds* (Pelham Books, London, 1987)
*Cattle* (Christopher Helm Publishers Ltd, 1991)

Quittet, E., & Richard, P. *Les Races Chevalines Françaises* (Ministère de l'Agriculture, Paris, 1953)

Quittet, E. *Les Races Bovines Françaises* (La Maison Rustique, Paris, 1963)
    *Les Races Ovines Françaises* (La Maison Rustique, Paris, 1965)

Rayns, F. 'Norfolk Horn Sheep', *J. Royal Agric. Soc.* 130 (1969)

Robertson, A., & Asker, A. A. 'The Genetic History and Breed Structure of British Friesian Cattle', *Empire J. of Exp. Agric.* 19 (1951)

Rosenberg, M. M. 'Fleece Colour in Crossbred Soay Sheep' (1977, private communication)
    'Weights of Hebridean, Shetland and Whitefaced Woodland Lambs' (1980, private communication)

Royle, N. J. 'Polymorphisms in Rare Breeds of Cattle' (PhD thesis, Reading, 1983)

Ruspoli, M. *The Caves of Lascaux* (Thames & Hudson, London, 1987)

Short, R. V. 'The Introduction of New Species of Animals for the Purpose of Domestication', *Sym. Zool. Soc. London* 40 (1976)

Sierra, I. *La Raza Ovina Salz* (Facultad Veterinaria, Zaragoza 1989)

Speed, J. G., & Speed, M. G. *The Exmoor Pony* (Countrywide Livestock Ltd, 1977)

Stanford, J. K. *British Friesians: A History of the Breed* (Parrish, London, 1956)

Stuart, Lord David. *An Illustrated History of Belted Cattle* (Scottish Academic Press, Edinburgh, 1970)

Symes, M. V. 'Achondroplasia in Cattle' (1981, private communication)

Tribe, D. E., & Tribe, E. M. 'North Ronaldsay Sheep', *Scottish Agriculture* 29 (1949)

Trow-Smith, R. *A History of British Livestock Husbandry* (Routledge & Kegan Paul, London, 2 vols, 1957, 1959)

Wagoner, D. M. (ed.) *Equine Genetics and Selection Procedures* (Equine Research Publications, Dallas, USA, 1978)

Wallace, R., & Watson, Sir J. A. S. *Farm Livestock of Great Britain* (Oliver & Boyd, Edinburgh, 5th ed., 1923)

Wallis, U. R. C. R. 'British Spotted Horses and Ponies' (1977, private communication)

Warriss, P. D., *et.al.* 'Lean Meat Quality in Different Pig Breed Types' (Paper to BSAP Winter Meeting, 1988)

Weiner, G. 'Breed Structure in the Pedigree Ayrshire Cattle Population in Great Britain', *J. Agric. Sci.* 43 (1953)

Werner, A. R. *An Enquiry into the Origin of Piebald or Jacob Sheep* (Countrywide Livestock Ltd, 1975)
    'Berlin Cattle and Munich Cattle', *The Ark* Vol. III, Nos. 2, 3 (1976)

Whitaker, A. H., & Rudge, M. R. *The Value of Feral Farm Animals in New Zealand* (NZ Department of Lands & Survey, 1976)

Whitehead, G. K. *The Ancient White Cattle of Britain and their Descendants* (Faber & Faber, London, 1953)

Willis, M. 'Genetic Variation in British Livestock' (1980, private communication)

Winters, L. M. *Animal Breeding* (John Wiley & Sons, New York, USA, 1952)

Wiseman, J. *A History of the British Pig* (Duckworth, London, 1986)

*The Ark* was published by Countrywide Livestock Ltd until 1980, thereafter by the Rare Breeds Survival Trust Ltd.

# INDEX